How to Create the Life You Want After 50

Second Edition

How to
Create the Life
You Want
After 50

Second Edition

**Includes over 200 tips, exercises,
and updated resources
for planning at midlife**

Sara Brown, Ph.D. and Joan S. Malling

Savvy Sisters Press
Ashland, Oregon

How to Create the Life You Want After 50
Second Edition
by Sara Brown and Joan S. Malling

Published by:
Savvy Sisters Press
478 Siskiyou Boulevard
Ashland, OR 97520-2135 U.S.A.
541-482-5561
http://www.savvychoices.com

ISBN, print edition: 978-0-9748900-1-2
First Edition, 2004
Second Edition 2008, revised

Library of Congress Control Number: 2003195037

Note: This publication contains the opinions and ideas of its authors. It is intended to provide helpful and informative material on the subject matter covered. It is sold with the understanding that the authors and publisher are not engaged in rendering professional services in the book. If the reader requires personal assistance or advice, a competent professional should be consulted.

The authors and publisher specifically disclaim any responsibility for any liability, loss, or risk, personal or otherwise, which is incurred as a consequence, directly or indirectly, of the use and application of any of the contents of this book.

The publisher offers discounts on this book when ordered in quantity.

For Neil and Paul

And special thanks to...

People who shared their lives with us through discussion, formal interviews, and in our workshops.

Friends and family who edited, proofread, and brainstormed with us, including Anne Dickason, Peter Gibb, Marybeth Kampman, Neil Malling, Angela Rinaldi, Paul Steinle, Julie Walton, and Charlyn Wilson.

Administrators at Southern Oregon University:
Aletha Lundblad, Barbara Scott, and Jeanne Stallman.

Jane Shaff, who continues to inspire Joan, and Carol Angel, who taught Sara how to plan.

Our team who put it together: Maureen Battistella (photo), Kim McLaughlin (cover), Rich Peck (photo), Joan Pinkert (layout), and Bob Smith (printing).

And all those who offered support and encouragement along the way.

Preface

Since 2004, when we first published How to Create the Life You Want After 50, we have conducted numerous "What's Next? Planning at Midlife" workshops, based on this book, for businesses, government agencies, and colleges.

The experiences of participants have reinforced our enthusiasm for presenting this planning process. Here are some examples. One workshop participant, Bill, was skeptical. For him, financial planning was the key to a happy retirement. By the close of the workshop Bill committed to using his financial resources to fulfill his important values and schedule a day once a quarter for both financial and life planning.

At another workshop, Jan confessed wistfully that as a young woman she had dreamed of being a professional musician. Life and responsibilities had intervened and she had given up on her dream. She used the material in chapter ten, creativity and learning, to help identify classes and activities to bring the pleasure of music back into her life.

And then there was Deborah, who was terrified of a blank "to-do" list. She was two years from retirement and couldn't imagine what she would do with her time once she wasn't working. She focused on how she might use her work-related skills in new ways and develop new friendships.

Workshop participants have ranged in age from 30 to 70. What they had in common was their belief that it's never too early or too late to plan for the life you want to live.

Sara and Joan, June 2007.

Contents

Exercises

Part One

Thriving at Midlife

This book is about *using the rest of your life to live with purpose and passion*. This book is for you if you are in your late 40s or older, and you want to create a plan to capitalize on the opportunities and issues that will be, or already are, affecting your life. This is a planning book for people at midlife.

Around 50, people start asking themselves, "What's next?" We, Sara Brown and Joan Malling, certainly have asked that question, as have our friends. One night, sitting around Joan's dining room table, we were talking about all the changes and uncertainties that occur during midlife. Both of us have spent the better part of our careers helping adults at mid-career plan their professional transitions. But that evening we realized the "What's next?" question at this age goes far beyond restlessness or dissatisfaction at work. People in their 40s, 50s, and 60s begin to recognize that life is finite. They begin to sort out relationships, assess family responsibilities, and try to figure out what they want to do with their time for the next 30 or more years.

We Gathered Stories

Our research, including interviews with 60 people age 45 and older, indicated that few people at midlife knew how to create a life plan. Most were emphatic that the choices their parents made at this age were not appropriate for them. But, they weren't sure how to map out a plan for themselves. Most importantly, we learned from the older people we interviewed that *life after 50 can be a time of rejuvenation rather than retirement*. Many felt that it could be a time of exploration, enjoyment, and accomplishment. We decided to write this book to help you plan how to create your life after 50 so that it's satisfying, meaningful and productive.

Everyone we interviewed said financial security was a critical part of his or her plans. We devote a chapter to financial security, but this is not a financial planning book. The questions we confront go beyond financial concerns:

- What's important to me?
- How can I live my life with purpose and passion?
- How do I want to spend my time?
- How can I further use and develop my skills and interests?
- How can my friendships be enriched?
- What are my family responsibilities, and how can I fulfill them and still make plans?
- How can I stay healthy and fit?

Our goal is to help you figure out the answers to these, and other, questions.

Your Savvy Sisters

We, Sara and Joan, are both in this life phase. And, between us, we have over 50 years' professional experience working in human resource management, career counseling, and adult education. Perhaps even more importantly, we have both recently made significant life changes.

Sara moved from Connecticut to Ashland, Oregon, taking her consulting business with her. The move was precipitated by an unexpected job opportunity for her husband, Paul, in Ashland, where they planned to retire eventually. Several years before the move, Sara and Paul bought a house in Ashland and were using it as rental property until the day they would move there. Though they had a long-range retirement plan, the decision to move earlier necessitated a careful analysis of their finances, family responsibilities, and lifestyle.

Joan and her husband, Neil, decided to rebalance their lives. After the death of a friend who loved to travel, they realized they shouldn't keep putting off their dream of living abroad part of each year. After trying out various locations during vacations, completing a financial review, and negotiating work commitments with their business partners, they bought a canal/river cruiser in Holland. Now they spend their summers on the inland waterways of Europe. Winters are spent in Portland, Oregon, working and catching up with friends and family.

Similar to many of you, we've both juggled our lives around our responsibilities for elderly parents—both our own and our husbands' parents. And we've both made it a priority to be involved in the lives of our children, grandchildren, nieces, and nephews.

Using our combined personal and professional experiences, and the stories of those we interviewed, we will talk with you as your *Savvy Sisters* in this book, as though we are sitting with you at your kitchen table offering tips, information, exercises to stimulate your thinking, and additional resources. But before we get started, we'd like to share some thoughts about why planning at midlife is different for us now than for past generations.

Changing the Rules

Our lives are strongly influenced by the expectations of parents and families, gender roles, and cultural and workplace attitudes—the "rules" we live by. Many of these rules have changed over the past 20 years. Baby boomers are accustomed to women working in jobs that were once closed to them, men staying home to care for the kids or earning less than their wives, and racial minorities no longer being restricted educationally or professionally. We helped change these rules, and now these changes affect how we feel about life after 50.

Our parents lived by the old rules, and the choices they made for life after 50 don't fit for us. At 50, most of our parents anticipated living only 20-25 more years with a few years of retirement leisure. But those of us who remain free of cancer and heart disease may live well into our 80s, 90s, or join the growing ranks of centenarians.

Our expectations about health, money, housing, and work differ from our parents' expectations. Recent surveys show the majority of people 50+ are searching for better work/life balance and want to continue working at least part time during their retirement years. Our generation wants to explore new options and take on new challenges. We are once again changing the rules.

What's in This Book?

How to Create the Life You Want After 50 guides you, chapter by chapter, through a three-step planning process.

1. We help you identify and assess typical midlife issues and opportunities.

2. We ask questions and provide exercises to help you clarify your needs and wants.

3. We provide ideas, information, and resources to help you develop your plan.

Along the way, key insights are indicated by a ❗; exercises by a 🏃.

Depending on your interests, you may read this book from cover to cover or pick and choose by topic. You may find the exercises useful; you may want to follow-up with the additional resources at the end of each chapter. We encourage you to highlight what seems most important to you or to record ideas in a separate journal. Most importantly, *do what works for you.*

Planning at midlife often begins with events or experiences that trigger the idea, "It's time I thought about what I want in the next phase of my life." *Part Two* analyzes these events or experiences that motivate us to begin planning how to change the course of our lives.

Part Three explores the unique, often spiritual, aspects of transitions at midlife and the benefits of optimism. An exercise to help you re-assess your life values is included.

Parts Four and Five are the "how to" sections. *Part Four* includes exercises to help you identify your interests, skills, and strengths. It offers practical ideas for your choices related to work, living space, community involvement, creativity, learning, and travel. *Part Five* examines the role of relationships in your life plan: friends, spouse or partner, and aging parents.

Part Six pulls it all together. The significant points of each chapter are synthesized in Chapter 15, Your Savvy Sisters Summarize. Chapter 16 includes worksheets to help you create *Your Life After 50 Plan*.

We will guide you in making your own choices to create a satisfying life within your budget. You may not be able to quit your job now, but you may be able to negotiate more flexible hours. You may not be able to erase those wrinkles, but you can start a new exercise program. You can decide to take a class or make new friends. Our goals are to prompt your thinking and experimentation, help you figure out what's important to you, and get you going on *Your Life After 50 Plan*. We want to help you live with purpose and passion for the rest of your life.

Now let's get started!

Part Two

Triggers
Life Events That Get Our Attention

All the people we interviewed told us about key experiences that got their attention and "triggered" a new awareness of the flow of their lives around 50.

The most forceful of these triggers were life-altering events such as being downsized and not being able to find a comparable job, suffering the death of a parent or good friend, or having an investment portfolio take a nose dive. More subtle events also acted as triggers: hair loss, wrinkles, and other physical changes; kids leaving home; or finding your home is too big for two people.

These attention-getting triggers—whether a jolt or a slower "Oh, yes, now I understand" insight—led to a transition phase of reflection and processing. The triggers were a wake-up call.

!

◉ A trigger is a key event, a life-altering experience, or a vivid insight that causes us to reconsider our lives. Often, reflecting on a trigger motivates us to begin planning how to change the course of our lives.

When we analyzed the triggers described by the 60 people we interviewed, we found that five were most frequently mentioned:

- Declining work satisfaction
- Concerns about financial security
- Changes in appearance and fitness
- Options for location and living space
- Serious illness or loss

The five chapters in Part Two focus on these triggers. We provide exercises in these chapters to help you think about and plan your responses to these events now or when you face them.

1

Dilbert Is Right
The Work Trigger

*When our jobs are more to us than just
a means of earning a living, our talents, preferences,
and true dispositions come to life.*
Marsha Sinetar

Dilbert, the underdog hero of cubicle dwellers everywhere, has endured the slings and arrows of office life since 1989 when Scott Adams created the comic strip. But what keeps Dilbert doing his job, anyway? Why doesn't he quit? Is there something Dilbert still hopes to get from his work that has eluded him?

Dilbert is popular because many of us identify with his foibles whether we like or dislike our job. Most of us enjoy our work and the social connections and/or feelings of productivity and usefulness that work can offer. But today we don't want to "just work." We want a work/life balance achieved through flexible hours, good benefits, respect, and a sense of purpose.

For some of us, burnout, layoffs, downsizing, rightsizing, and the glass ceiling are the realities of today's work world. Organizations are flatter, and there is less room for advancement in mid- to late-career. Also, at midlife we may question our energy and our ability to be competitive in the job market if we quit our present jobs. Yet, we still want to "accomplish" something more, whatever that may be. Dilbert doesn't quit working, and many of us apparently don't want to, or can't afford to, quit either.

The work triggers that may occur in our lives around 50—a desire for better work/life balance, a realization that our self-worth is based on our role at work, job elimination, dwindling job satisfaction, or a choice between job security and a "last hurrah"—require us to rethink our personal and professional values and goals. For many it is also a time to ask ourselves if we have contributed something to society, to our profession, or to our family that will endure and will provide a legacy for us and for others.

Work and Self-worth—Susan's Story

Susan had a career as an educator, a high school teacher, and an administrator. At 55, after 27 years with a school district, she took early retirement. She had no intention of quitting work, but reorganization eliminated the department she was heading. Since she was dissatisfied with the leadership of the organization and figured if she stayed history would repeat itself, she found part-time work and announced her retirement. In retrospect, she realizes she was tired and hoped the part-time job would give her time to rest and explore her options. Instead, for the next five years, she went from one work project to another and sat on several nonprofit boards. She never took the time to sort out what she really wanted from work.

The funding for her current project ended recently, and Susan finds herself back in a decision mode. She says she got a "knot in her stomach" when she learned the project would end. She fears its ending will leave a hole in her life. The prospect of not having a job scares her, but she has still avoided taking the time to sort out what she wants from work. Susan questions whether she has energy for something new. She also wonders whether her concerns are based on limited energy or ambivalence about working. Susan acknowledges that for her the question of "What will I do?" is not really a financial question, but a psychological one: "Am I still worthwhile if I'm not working?"

Lessons from Susan

Susan's story illustrates how many of us need to rethink what work means to us at midlife. We must redefine work's meaning for our current identities and lives. She successfully navigated the first midlife trigger event related to work—the reorganization that inspired her to quit—by retiring and repackaging herself as a consultant in her career field. Now, Susan is in the throes of her second midlife trigger event—the questioning of her self-worth if she doesn't have a job. What seemed at first like just another career transition is actually a life transition. Susan realizes that what she wants in life has changed, and not all of what she wants is related to work.

The psychologist Erik Erickson said that self-worth for many adults "consists entirely in *what they are doing*," and not in who they are.

> **!** If you can't separate what you do from who you are, you're particularly vulnerable to stress and disappointment because there is much in the work world we can't control. Take time at midlife to get reacquainted with your self.

As we think about the role we want work to play in our lives after 50, like Susan, we may need to assess our psychological and financial needs as well as our energy level. Once we do that, we'll be in a better position to develop new work goals.

Work/Life Balance—Ben's Story

Since high school Ben has seen his life proceeding along five major tracks: career, hobby, community, religion, and family. Over the years the balance among the five has shifted. Each shift required a transition from one set of priorities to another. For example, his hobbies and religious activities consumed his attention when he was young. After getting married his priorities became tending his growing family and his career. When his sons left home his priorities shifted again. With more time for volunteering in the community, he helped out in a seniors' program and volunteered for hospice work.

A recent leave of absence has given Ben time for more active consideration of his career and life options. He's trying to decide if he should start a new career project or expand the many other parts of his life and let the career part "cruise."

Ben's trigger has been the slow realization that during the last ten years he has not excelled in the way he previously had. He worries that he won't have the stamina to launch a new career project and achieve in the same way he did in the past. When reflecting on the various stages of his career, Ben remembers that for each new stage and project he took on, there was a great deal of energy, pain, and tension involved. He's not sure he wants to, or could, go through that again.

Lessons from Ben

Ben is grappling with his readiness to change his life. At 56, he's in transition again—figuring out where he wants to direct his energy to effectively balance the five tracks of his life. His story points out that a variety of interests and experiences give us more choices. When one road is blocked, another road can be taken.

Betty Friedan in *The Fountain of Age* writes about women between the ages of 50 and 60 who returned to work, started careers after their children entered school, or who combined homemaking and work. They all enjoyed higher life satisfaction compared to women or men in a single, continuous role.

> **!** 🔍 Having multiple paid and unpaid roles may help us become less dependent on our jobs and salary as a gauge of our worth or identity. But if we don't periodically rebalance the mix of activities in our lives, an abundance of roles may also make us feel over committed and burned out.

Weighing Choices—Hiro's Story

Hiro was content. In his late 40s, Hiro was the managing partner of a law firm. He enjoyed his work and felt loyal to the firm and his colleagues. Hiro and his wife had saved money for their two children's education and had a secure investment portfolio. He was approached recently by a group of investors who wanted him to head up a new business venture. This opportunity has triggered his reassessment of work.

If Hiro accepts this opportunity, he will be working with people younger than himself. Like Susan and Ben, Hiro wonders if he has the energy to keep up with his new colleagues; leading a start-up will require long hours and create stress. He doesn't want to rob his wife and children of his participation in their family life. He's also concerned about putting his personal finances in jeopardy if the business isn't successful.

Despite these concerns, Hiro is intrigued and surprised at the excitement he feels about the prospect of creating a new business. He thinks this could be his "last, big hurrah," a legacy he could leave behind, and he feels up to the challenge.

Lessons from Hiro

Hiro is not dissatisfied with his current job but acknowledges that he has an unrealized entrepreneurial itch. Creating a new company appeals to him; he thinks it could serve as his professional legacy.

Hiro's story points out that there is often a price to be paid when choices are made—trade-offs such as time away from his family or a loss of financial security. His story also illustrates that an opportunity to create a professional legacy can be a powerful life trigger.

Work Triggers

Susan, Ben, and Hiro all have choices to make. Susan and Ben have had successful careers. They now question if they still have what it takes, or want to do what it takes, to excel and compete in the same type of work. Hiro is at the peak of his career, and he can either enjoy the status and security he's achieved, or he can grab what he thinks might be his last chance to shape a new company.

All three stories demonstrate the tensions and ambivalence that face us as we make career-altering choices at midlife. All three, for different reasons, question if they have what it takes for the next phase of their work life. Ben, Susan, and Hiro don't have role models for this transition—few people do.

Your Savvy Sisters' Advice

- Manage yourself. You must take responsibility for your own career. The worlds of work and society aren't set up to help us plan our lives.

- Develop your own plan for a satisfying life, based on your own self-understanding. No one else can define what is important to you.

- Experiment by exploring new interests. They will help define the future you.

- Develop a positive outlook and set goals to redirect your work life. Your stamina will increase as you take charge of your life.

- Remember that there is no arbitrary cutoff age for creativity and growth.

exercise▶
Redefining Success

If you are at a life transition now, not just at a point where you want to change your job, you may need to redefine your benchmarks for success and create some new options.

exercise▸

Redefining Success

Start with some very basic questions about work:

• What do you really like doing?

• What do you think is worth doing?

• What challenges you?

• How important is income to you?

• If you want to create a legacy for others,
  what will that legacy be?

If you have experienced a job or career transition,
you may have gone through the analysis it takes to
make a work change. That experience will be useful to
you now because you have already considered what's
important to you and where your strengths lie. If you'd
like to update this information, you'll find the Midlife
Transitions Inventory in Part Four to help you identify
your interests and strengths. You may want to complete
the inventory now.

Resources to Help You Think About Your Work Triggers

Books

Bronson, Po. *What Should I Do with My Life?* New York: Random House, 2002.

Covey, Stephen. *The 8th Habit: From Effectiveness to Greatness.* New York: Free Press, 2004.

Erikson, Erik. *Identity and the Life Cycle.* New York: W. W. Norton & Company, 1980.

Freedman, M. and Harris, A. *Encore: Finding Work That Matters in the Second Half of Life.* New York: Public Affairs, 2007.

Goldberg, Beverly. *Age Works: What Corporate America Must Do to Survive the Graying of the Workforce.* New York: The Free Press, 2000.

Hakim, Cliff. *We are All Self-Employed: How to Take Control of Your Career.* San Francisco: Berrett-Koehler Publishers, 2003.

Kay, Andrea. *Life's a Bitch and Then You Change Careers: 9 Steps to Get Out of Your Funk and on to Your Future.* New York: Harry N. Abrams, 2005.

Kaye, Beverly and Jordan-Evans, Sharon. *Love It, Don't Leave It: 26 Ways to Get What You Want at Work.* San Francisco: Berrett-Koehler Publishers, 2003.

Sadler, William. *The Third Age: 6 Principles of Growth and Renewal after Forty.* Cambridge, MA: Perseus Books, 2000.

Sinetar, Marsha. *Do What You Love and the Money Will Follow: Discovering Your Right Livelihood.* New York: Dell Publishing, 1987.

Whyte, David. *Crossing the Unknown Sea: Work as a Pilgrimage of Identity.* New York: Riverhead Books, 2001.

Am I still worthwhile if I'm not working?

From Susan's story

2

The 55/62 Plan
The Financial Security Trigger

There are risks and costs to a program of action.
But they are far less than the long-range risks and costs
of comfortable inaction.
John F. Kennedy

Do you wish you had the financial security to try something new in your work or life? Do you have a financial nest egg but wish it were bigger? Or, do you have a deep down fear of not having "enough"?

Some people systematically plan for financial security and independence. For others, a friend's retirement, a downturn in the stock market or receiving a disappointing 401K statement may trigger the question: "Do I have enough money?" Or, more to the point, "Could I afford to live comfortably, however I define 'comfortable,' if I weren't working?" And, if these questions spur you on to consider your balance sheet more closely, you might as well think about what you will do with your life when you are financially independent.

A secure financial base was a bedrock goal for the 60 people we interviewed. Some had experienced a specific event that triggered financial planning; others had a lifelong commitment to financial security. Those who were retired believed they had sufficient funds to live on, even if just modestly. Those in their 40s and 50s who were still working had not achieved their financial goals, but many had a plan for getting there. Some were much further along than others.

Creating a Financial Plan—Theron's Story

Theron is the oldest of 18 children, and maybe that's why having enough money to live on has always been important to him. At 40 he retired from the Marines with a small pension and $30,000, which provided seed money for a financial savings plan. Today, at 59, he and his wife, Elizabeth, have acquired a sizable financial nest egg, which Theron attributes to their "55/62 plan." Elizabeth will be 55 when Theron is 62. At 62 he doesn't want to retire from his work as a human resources consultant, but he wants to be financially independent. "If I want to work, I will," Theron says, "but I won't have to because it won't impact my ability to meet my financial obligations."

To achieve their 55/62 plan, Theron and Elizabeth have been saving 30 percent of their income. In addition, they tithe ten percent to their church. To make their plan more than wishful thinking, they created a budget. Using a spreadsheet, Theron keeps track of every penny they spend. Their plan requires them to agree on big purchases. They have quarterly dinner table meetings to discuss their investing and spending activities. While they are close now to meeting their 55/62 plan goals, the uncertainty of the stock market is acting as a trigger for Theron, and he wants to acquire a "greater cushion."

Lessons from Theron

Even for those of us who aren't as disciplined about saving and investing as Theron and Elizabeth are, Theron's story points out how important it is to have a financial goal, know the difference between what you "want" and what you "need," and live within a budget. Theron's story also illustrates that we differ widely in how we approach and answer the question, "Do I have enough money?"

The value of a plan was reinforced in *Money Magazine's* "The Great American Wealth Test." The net worth of "high planners," people who plan routinely, is almost 20 percent higher than those who rarely plan.

> ❗ ◈ There is a connection between the *habit* of monitoring your saving and spending and accruing increased wealth.

Theron's goal of financial independence also includes working in a job he likes, even after achieving financial security. Many boomers who say they want to work whether or not they're financially secure share this goal.

While Theron is a model for disciplined financial planning, Linda's story is a cautionary tale about what can happen if we don't plan.

Sticking to a Plan—Linda's Story

Linda, 55 and divorced, fears she'll become a bag lady. She's afraid of living past the time she can take care of herself financially. She believes she should be saving money but hasn't been able to stick with the plan she developed at a retirement seminar.

"They gave us a plan for how to pay off all our bills in seven years, and I ran the spread sheets on it and figured out how to do it," she says.

Linda stuck to her plan for a year, but then things got hectic at work, and "I fell out of taking care of myself financially and physically." Although she doesn't know when or how she'll do it, she hopes to get back to her plan so she can pay down the mortgage on her house, sell it, and move to a condominium.

Linda has the additional concern of job security because she's the oldest person in her high tech company. She's afraid she won't be able to keep up with younger employees and might be a candidate for downsizing.

Lessons from Linda

Linda's story points out that you may experience several "triggers"—for Linda they were the fear of living past the time she can take care of herself financially and the fear of losing her job—before you take substantive action toward financial security.

Linda is not alone in her fears. MetLife's recent "Retirement and Savings Study" indicates that 79 percent of the employees surveyed are worried they'll outlive their savings and will need to work during retirement. Yet, 67 percent say they are behind in their savings or haven't started to save yet.

We all have crises that throw us off track temporarily, but if we wait for our lives to be uncomplicated, we'll never create or stick to our plans. It may take a work or health crisis before Linda is sufficiently motivated to stick to her plan and move forward. The lesson of Linda's story is: Don't wait to plan, and get right back to your plan if you get temporarily derailed.

> **!**
> ◉ Attaining financial security requires steady, habitual attention to a financial plan.

Your Savvy Sisters' Advice

Admit it: Financial security is bedrock. While money can't ensure happiness, your options are increased if financial security is the foundation of your life plan.

- Identify your priorities now and for the later date when you're shooting for financial independence.
- Figure out what you need for financial security and independence now and in the future.
- Determine what your financial resources are, including your company's benefits, if any.
- Develop an investment strategy, balancing risk exposure with return potential.
- Determine your needs for insurance, tax guidance, and estate planning.
- Start tracking your progress.
- Keep revising your financial plan as you make new decisions for your life after 50.

Taking the First Steps

If reading this chapter has been a trigger for you, the first steps to your financial security and independence should include an analysis of your current financial needs and your monthly income. You will then want to start analyzing your future financial needs and income. As you create Your Life After 50 Plan, you may need to modify these initial figures. Your Savvy Sisters are here to tell you that you can't do it any other way, as tedious as the process is. Worksheets to help you are at the end of this chapter.

Once you've gotten this process underway, you may want to consult a financial planner or use financial planning software to help you with the "What ifs": "What if

I haven't saved enough to fund my kids' college expenses?" "My retirement income is tied to the stock market's performance—what if the market drops?" "What if I want to travel extensively?" "What if I decide to take an early retirement buy out?" "What if I want to start my own business?" One of the most significant benefits of using computerized planners is that they help you understand the effects of inflation and return on investment.

See Resources at the end of this chapter for specific suggestions.

Financial Needs

In the analysis of your financial needs, consider two time periods: current and future. What are your current expenses? What will your expenses be in the future? We encourage you to estimate your current expenses now and to project future expenses as Your Life After 50 Plan develops.

For example, if you currently have a long commute to work and you're considering changing jobs or working from home, your automobile costs may change. If you have more available time, your leisure or travel expenses may increase. If you plan to work part time or quit working, be sure to include the cost of benefits you might be receiving at work such as health and life insurance.

Current and Future Expenses Worksheet

Your Savvy Sisters want you to be financially secure as you make changes in your income or expenses. The following analysis is necessary to reach that goal.

To begin, fill in your estimates for each category of your current expenses. Then think about what your future expenses in each category might be. You may want to fill in your initial ideas for the future. However, you will need to come back to this exercise to modify (or fill in) this column when you know more about Your Life After 50 Plan.

exercise►

Current and Future Expenses Worksheet

Regular Monthly Expense Categories	Current Expenses	Future Expenses
Mortgage or rent		
Food		
Utilities		
Telephone		
Cable		
Online service		
Health insurance		
Life insurance		
Long-term care insurance		
Auto insurance		
Auto expenses		
Transportation		
Education		
Loans or credit cards		
Clothing		
Entertainment		
Services: lawn, house cleaning, dry cleaning		
Contributions		
Personal care		
Other		
Subtotal	$	$

Periodic Expense Categories to be Prorated by Month	Current Expenses	Future Expenses
Vacations		
House maintenance		
Major home improvements		
Gifts		
Taxes		
Legal and accounting services		
New auto		
Uninsured medical and dental		
Veterinarian		
Other		
Subtotal	$	$
Total Monthly Expenses	$	$

Financial Resources

Now that you have an idea of your current expenses and you are starting to think about what your expenses might be in the future, consider your current and projected sources of monthly income by completing the next exercise.

exercise▶

Current and Future Income Worksheet

The following worksheet will help you explore your options for meeting the expenses projected in your Current and Future Expenses Worksheet.

exercise▸

Current and Future Income Worksheet

Source of Income	Current Monthly Income	Current Periodic Income— Prorated by Month	Future Monthly Income	Future Periodic Income— Prorated by Month	When will this income be available? How long will it last?
Stocks and bonds					
Pension					
IRA's/other tax deferred accounts					
Insurance					
Social security					
Bank and credit union accounts					
Income property (minus expenses)					
Sale of assets: boat, house, car, other					
Earned income					
Other					
Total Monthly Income	$	$	$	$	

The two worksheets you just completed are only a beginning (sorry!), but they can help you determine if Your Life After 50 Plan is financially realistic. Your Savvy Sisters strongly recommend that you now go to the next step. Make an appointment with a financial counselor or experiment with a financial planning software program to firm up your plan.

Resources to Help You Get Started on Your Financial Plan

Books

Bach, David. *Smart Women Finish Rich*. New York: Broadway Books, 2002.

Clyatt, Bob. *Work Less, Live More*. Berkeley: Nolo, 2005.

Dominguez, Joe and Robin, Vicki. *Your Money or Your Life*. New York: Penguin Books, 1992.

Farrell, Mary. *Beyond the Basics*. New York: Simon & Schuster, 2000.

Gardner, Tom and David. *The Motley Fools Money After 40*. New York: Fireside Books, 2004.

Orman, Suze. *The Road to Wealth*. New York: Riverhead Books, 2001.

Quinn, Jane Bryant. *Smart and Simple Financial Strategies*. New York: Simon & Schuster, 2006.

Schwab, Charles R. *You're Fifty—Now What? Investing for the Second Half of Your Life*. New York: Crown Publishers, 2001.

Slesnick, Twila and Suttle, John C. *IRA's, 401(k)s, and Other Retirement Plans Taking Your Money Out*. Berkeley: Nolo, 2006.

Websites

- www.kiplinger.com
- http://money.cnn.com

3

After 50, It's Patch, Patch, Patch
The Appearance and Fitness Trigger

Gray hair is God's graffiti.
Bill Cosby

Crumbs from our 50th birthday cake are no sooner swept away than we notice subtle signs that our bodies are heading south. We can no longer read the phone book unaided, and we must either hold all printed material at arm's length or stock up on drug store glasses to place in strategic spots around the house. We frequently ask others to stop mumbling and repeat themselves. And although we've always been fit, rising "bad" cholesterol scores suddenly plague us.

My Generation magazine reported that when playwright Sam Shepard turned 50, he reflected on the question of age. Forty was hard, but by 50 he was "cruising." When he turned 59 he was asked if he was still cruisin' along. "In overdrive," he laughed. "It's very strange what happens with the body—[it's] not as easy to swing up on a horse anymore."

These changes in our bodies are nature's way of telling us we're aging. They are triggers that cause us to consider how we take care of ourselves. They challenge us to examine the meaning we give to graying hair and thickening waistlines. But what if we're not ready for such self-scrutiny? What if our professional or social lives or our self-image aren't in synch with this annoying deterioration? Some of us head for the vitamin counter, others enroll at the YMCA, and some consider a plastic surgeon.

Putting Vanity Aside—Your Savvy Sister Sara's Story

My mother has a serious hearing loss, and I've known since I was in my 30s that I also have a hearing problem that would gradually worsen. Since my mother refuses to wear her hearing aids, everyone has to shout or just give up talking to her. I didn't want that to happen to me, so I made my children promise to tell me when it was time to get professional help, in case I didn't notice.

Over time my hearing got gradually worse, and I frequently had to ask people to speak louder. At business meetings I arrived early and sat close to the speaker. I knew I needed hearing aids, so I started talking to people about the process. I discussed it with my hairdresser. He told me how he would cut my hair so my ears wouldn't show, and I felt better. Yet, I kept finding excuses for not getting them.

To me, hearing aids were an undeniable symbol of old age. Stern lectures from women friends who wore aids, whom I didn't consider "old," failed to convince me I wouldn't look old if I wore them. What finally motivated me was attending a weeklong conference where I had no control over the seating arrangement. I came home exhausted from the strain of trying to hear and immediately made an appointment with an audiologist.

I'm now the proud owner of hearing aids so small I don't worry if my ears show. I decided that being able to hear was far more attractive than saying "Huh?" or "Would you repeat that?"

Lessons from Sara

Sara believed she would look old if she wore hearing aids. Even though she had evidence to the contrary—professional women friends who were not diminished because of hearing aids—her fears caused her to live unnecessarily with a disability that could be corrected. Once she had hearing aids she realized she'd worried for nothing. Her friends reinforced the fact that the hearing aids didn't age her. In fact, most people didn't realize she was wearing them.

> ◉ In our youth-loving culture, physical signs of aging may be detrimental to one's career or self-image. That leaves us with some choices. We can correct what is correctable: hearing, vision, hair, and weight; accept and enjoy our hard-earned maturity; and confront the stereotypes of physical aging. Or, we can decide not to care.

Stay Fit but Understand Your Limits—Betsy's Story

Betsy has just celebrated her 60th birthday by taking a family sailing trip. Tennis, scuba diving, and travel are her passions. She's also developing a consulting practice that requires her to travel extensively. Betsy rarely sits still. She believes the quality of her life will be diminished if she isn't physically active. But to be active she needs to maintain her energy and strength.

At 60 she's concerned about regaining muscle strength and flexibility. "My muscles are cranky. They hurt more," she says.

Over the last four years Betsy made two coast-to-coast moves and suffered the death of her husband. She knows she paid a price for that stress. "I figure that with all the changes and tensions of the last four years, it was in my muscles where the strain came out." Chronic shoulder and right arm pain from using her computer also bother her.

Betsy is experiencing a conflict between her wish to maintain a physically vigorous life and her growing awareness of her physical limitations and diminished energy. This conflict has been a trigger for Betsy to examine her body's needs and determine if, and how, she can continue at the same pace she did as a younger woman. She now realizes that developing and implementing a fitness plan is key to staying physically active.

We asked Betsy what she would have projected for her health if we'd asked her when she was 50. "Oh, I think I would have been in denial," she says. "At that point I was very physically active: scuba diving, playing tennis and a lot of golf. I would have been in denial that anything would happen to me."

Sitting at 60, looking toward 70, Betsy is optimistic about the future based on her mother's life. "I've looked at pictures of my mother at 86 where we were playing golf. There's nothing that says I shouldn't be equally strong and physically active."

Lessons from Betsy

At 50, Betsy was in denial that aging could slow her down. She took fitness for granted and overtaxed her body. It didn't occur to her to plan for a time when she had to work at maintaining general good health. Stiff muscles and diminished energy were triggers for Betsy to decide to develop a fitness plan. She realized that if she were to be playing golf at 86, as her mother did, she would need to make fitness a permanent way of life.

Neither Betsy nor Sara decided to act on their awareness immediately. They both resisted taking action until their situations (lack of energy and hearing loss) were serious enough they couldn't deny them. Even after they acknowledged that action was needed, they both required more time (and suffering!) to develop a plan and act on it.

> ❗
> ◉ Responding to the triggers that eventually lead to change is rarely a straightforward process. Unfortunately, awareness alone is often not enough to motivate change. *Deciding* to develop a fitness plan is a few critical steps short of *having* a fitness plan and actually being fit.

People tend to lurch and zigzag toward change through a series of phases. Once you are able to go from the awareness stage to the planning stage, the support of others (friends, Weight Watchers, classes, etc.) will help you achieve your goals.

Lifestyles

On average, baby boomers, aided by science, can expect to live healthier and longer lives than their parents. How much longer depends partially on a number of lifestyle factors such as adequate exercise, sound nutrition, and whether or not we smoke or drink. Check Resources at the end of the chapter for websites with quizzes to estimate how long you're likely to live based on your lifestyle.

If you shun exercise, you used to be called a couch potato. Unfortunately, there's more at stake from sitting on the couch than a low self-image. With obesity and diabetes on the rise—obesity has doubled in the last 20 years and Type 2 diabetes increased by 33 percent in the 1990s—a sedentary lifestyle has been given a more intimidating (and hopefully motivating) name: Sedentary Death Syndrome.

Fortunately, many boomers are getting off the couch. Exercisers over 55 are the fastest-growing age group in health clubs. According to a study conducted by the International Health, Racquet & Sportsclub, the number of Americans over the age of 55 who belong to a gym grew 380 percent between 1987 and 2000.

Your Savvy Sisters' Advice

- Recognize that everyone's body changes after 50 (if not before).
- Exercise, exercise. If you don't use it, you *will* lose it!
- Warm up before exercising. Muscle tissue becomes less flexible with age. Take a few minutes to walk before slowly stretching your back and legs.
- Learn to relax. Experiment with techniques such as deep breathing, meditation, or yoga to find a method of relaxation to practice regularly.
- Do something about your hearing or vision, if you're having trouble. A hearing loss is more noticeable to other people than hearing aids will be. Ditto for glasses.
- Improve your appearance, if it will make you feel better. Hair coloring, hair replacement therapy, and/or cosmetic surgery may give you a psychological boost.
- Stop smoking and, if you drink alcohol, drink moderately.
- Eat a nutritious diet. Yes, you are what you eat.
- Discuss gender-related changes (menopause, impotence) with your doctor. Determine if medication is right for you.

Resiliency Factors

Boomers lead busy lives and juggling the demands of work and family can be stressful. Excessive stress can trigger the breakdown of both physical and mental health and speed the aging process. Adults with "psychological resiliency" age more slowly, says Al Siebert, author of *The Survivor Personality*.

Studies show that one's attitudes toward work and life events can improve overall health and significantly reduce the negative effects of stress. We'll talk more optimism in Chapter 7.

Healthy Living Quiz

Consider the following statements to determine if you are on your way to developing the attitudes that lead to a longer, healthier life.

exercise▶

Healthy Living Quiz

	How true is the statement for you? Rate 1 to 10; 10 = Always True
1. I regularly practice relaxation techniques.	
2. I regularly eat a nutritionally balanced diet.	
3. I consistently exercise three or more days a week, including stretching, aerobic, and weight bearing exercises.	
4. I seek the advice of health care practitioners to use appropriate medications and treatments.	
5. I believe that my attitude of commitment to the world and myself helps me cope with stress and transform it into something that promotes growth.	
6. I believe that if I try, I can positively influence much of what happens in my life.	
7. I see myself as being capable of solving problems and conflicts.	
8. I believe that feelings of powerlessness and passivity waste my life's opportunities.	
9. I believe that almost everything that happens to me, whether positive or negative, can be an opportunity for new learning and growth.	
10. I believe that personal growth leads to fulfillment.	
11. I have people in my life who support, encourage, and assist me in solving the problems I encounter.	

- Circle the statements you rated "5" or less.
- If an improvement in one of these areas would increase your health and well-being, what steps could you take now? See Resources for ideas.

Every day our bodies change and age. It is the process of life. Okay, so the pace of change seems to pick up when we hit 50. But, "patch, patch" can either become an unhealthy preoccupation or a trigger for planning and maintaining a healthy lifestyle.

Resources to Help You Plan and Maintain a Healthy Lifestyle

Books

Francina, Suza. *The New Yoga for People Over 50.* Deerfield Beech, FL: Health Communications, Inc., 1997.

Kabat-Zinn, Jon. *Full Catastrophe Living: Using the Wisdom of Your Body and Mind to Face Stress, Pain, and Illness.* New York: Dell Publishing, 1990.

Northrup, Christine, M.D. *Women's Bodies, Women's Wisdom.* New York: Bantam Books, 1998.

Northrup, Christine, M.D. *The Wisdom of Menopause.* New York: Bantam Books, 2001.

Peeke, Pamela. *Body for Life for Women.* Emmaus, PA: Rodale Press, 2005.

Phillips, Bill. *Body for Life.* New York: HarperCollins Publishing, 1999. (Exercise and physical conditioning programs for men and women of all ages.)

Roizen, Michael and Mehmet Oz. *YOU: The Owner's Manual: An Insider's Guide to the Body that Will Make You Healthier and Younger.* New York: Harper Collins Publishing, 2005. (Fun, informative, preventative health book.)

Small, Gary. *The Memory Bible: An Innovative Strategy for Keeping Your Brain Young.* New York: Hyperion, 2002.

Snowdon, David. *Aging with Grace: What the Nun Study Teaches Us About Leading Longer, Healthier, and*

More Meaningful Lives. New York: Bantam Books, 2001.

Valliant, George E. *Aging Well: Surprising Guideposts to a Happier Life from the Landmark Harvard Study of Adult Development.* Boston: Little Brown, 2002. (Long-term study of people now in their 70s shows that some lifestyle changes are more important than others.)

Weil, Andrew. *Healthy Aging: A Lifelong Guide to Your Physical and Spiritual Well-being.* New York: Alfred A. Knopt, 2005. (Diet, activity, and attitude.)

Yee, Rodney. *Moving Toward Balance: 8 Weeks of Yoga with Rodney Yee.* Emmaus, PA: Rodale Press, 2004.

Videotapes

Nelson, Miriam. *Strong Women Stay Young.* Produced by Women First Health Care, 1998. (Weight training program for women.) See www.strongwomen.com. Also available in book form.

Websites

- www.aad.org
  Learn about the causes and treatments for hair loss, as well as other dermatological topics, through the American Academy of Dermatology.

- www.aarp.magazine.org
  American Association of Retired Persons (AARP) publishers of *AARP The Magazine.*

- www.cosmeticsurgery.org
  Learn about procedures, choosing a surgeon, plus additional resources.

- www.eyemdlink.com
  A website dedicated to the education of the eye care consumer.

- www.healthandage.com
  Interactive health information for people as they
  move towards their senior years.
- www.health.harvard.edu
  Harvard Medical School gives advice for a healthier
  life, including gender specific health watches.
- www.health.nih.gov
  National Institutes of Health lists health topics,
  including a section on healthy lifestyles.
- www.healthyhearing.com
  Helpful information on hearing loss, hearing aids,
  etc.
- www.mayoclinic.com
  The Mayo Clinic provides resources to help you and
  your family stay healthy.
- www.resiliencycenter.com
  Learn about the relationship of resilience and
  longevity.

I've looked at pictures of my mother at 86
where we were playing golf. There's nothing that says
I shouldn't be equally strong and physically active.

From Betsy's story

4

Location, Location, Location
The Right Place and Space Trigger

A good home must be made, not bought.
Joyce Maynard

Should we stay put or move? After 50, issues such as the cost of living, weather, and lifestyle start us thinking about relocation.

We may yearn for a stronger sense of community. We may need an extra room for an office or space for projects. Many of us start questioning whether we want to stay in the same house or the same town. We start thinking about the kind of space we want for our living environment. This may be the first time our careers or children don't mandate where or how we live. We ask ourselves if we still want to take care of a four-bedroom house and yard.

Our triggers related to place and space are often closely tied to other triggers such as rethinking work or children leaving home, as Annie's story illustrates.

A Change of Focus—Annie's Story

As soon as Annie's daughter, Jessica, got her driver's license, Annie realized that her life would no longer be as child-focused as it had been for the previous 16 years. Two years later, just before leaving for college, Jessica decided to put away her childhood treasures and suggested changing her room to make it more comfortable for guests. Annie and Jessica worked together on the guest room conversion. Annie calls it a "rite of passage for both of us." She says it was "a tangible symbol of the change in both our lives." The conversion of Jessica's room reinforced Annie's understanding of the changes occurring in her life. With her daughter away at school, Annie now has more time to spend on her new interests, gardening and photography.

Lessons from Annie

The room conversion was an important step for Annie. Sometimes what we think of as a small change to our living environment can have a significant effect on how we perceive our lives. Annie realized that the transition of her daughter's childhood room to a guest room had a symbolic impact on both of them. For Annie, it reinforced her awareness of her daughter's independence and Jessica's reduced need for her time.

Finding a Community—Judy and Nate's Story

Judy and Nate spent their married lives moving. As a result of Nate's work, they lived in Egypt and several Latin American countries. Judy calls herself a "foreign service spouse." She was usually able to find work as a writer or editor wherever Nate's career with the US Agency for International Development (USAID) sent them. During the last three years of his work with USAID, they lived in Washington, D.C.

Judy and Nate knew they didn't want to live internationally or stay in Washington indefinitely. Both enjoyed
the excitement of life abroad and in the capitol, but they
yearned for a place with both a sense of community and
good medical facilities. Judy felt Washington didn't offer
a "sense of belonging," and Nate wasn't confident about
the quality of medical care available to them overseas.
He had developed cancer while living internationally and
knew the importance of a good medical facility.

When Nate took early retirement in his mid-fifties,
several decisions followed. Nate wanted to continue
working part time, and they wanted to relocate. They
also decided they wanted their next move to be to the
place where they'd retire.

Judy and Nate decided to take an exploratory trip to
places that appealed to them as a future home. Armed
with a book on retirement locations, they prepared an
itinerary, packed up their VW camper, and headed out.
Judy felt that spending time in the places of greatest
interest would help her make a final decision.

Judy and Nate fell in love with the weather, beauty,
and community spirit of a small, Western town during
this summertime visit. They put a bid on a house, but it
was rejected. That next winter they returned and realized
they were lucky their bid hadn't been accepted. The house
had a very steep driveway that was quite hazardous in
the ice and snow. During this visit they bought a lot and
had a house built. They're living comfortably in their
new house now, but it cost more than they'd expected. Nate
is concerned that the cost of maintenance may force them
to sell.

Lessons from Judy and Nate

Judy and Nate took three important steps: They
identified what was important to them, surveyed a variety

of options, and visited their favorite location at various seasons of the year.

However, they didn't put as much effort as they should have into assessing the pros and cons of various housing features based on the unfamiliar climate. They might have gotten advice from a local general contractor and spoken with their prospective neighbors about the impact of the climate. Also, they may have overestimated what they could afford and might have benefited from a session with a CPA or financial planner.

> **!**
>
> ◉ For many people, absence of the support of family, friends, or community may be the deciding factor whether to stay put or move. Renting for a year before you make a permanent move will give you time to see if you can create a satisfactory support system in a new location. You might also learn that you underestimated how much you'd miss the people where you live now.

Changing Needs Over Our Life Span—Liz's Story

Liz, a vibrant, single woman in her 70s, has moved several times in the last 12 years. Location preferences and space needs were deciding factors in each of these moves. Each place was right for the stage she was in at the time.

When she was in her early 60s, Liz and her husband lived and worked in San Diego, California. A trip to Asia caused them to reassess what was important in their lives. Burned out with their careers, they decided they'd be happier in a smaller, less stressful town. So, leaving their full-time careers, they moved to the small coastal town of Mendocino and built a large house.

Seven years later, Liz's husband died. Because there was a "couples' culture" in Mendocino, she decided to look for another town where there were more singles. It was a traumatic time, but she realized she "didn't have to be *stuck* in a place"; she could find a place to live that was better suited to her needs as a single woman. She was attracted to Ashland, Oregon's peaceful atmosphere, the support of family members who lived close by, and Ashland's world-class cultural events. Access to the good health care facilities available in the area was also a draw, so she rented a house in Ashland.

Liz recently moved again: this time to a high-rise apartment in a retirement community. She likes the location and the view and feels she'll be happy there for many years. Space was her biggest concern in making this move from a house to an apartment. An apartment needed to accommodate her piano and huge collection of books, and this one does. Books are necessary for her ongoing professional work as a translator and her general enjoyment of life.

Lessons from Liz

Over the years Liz's needs changed. She recognized that the place where she lived was important to her, and that her "quality of life could be equally right and interesting" in each place. By moving to Ashland, she optimized what was most important to her at the time: quality of life for a single woman, landscape, health care, and cultural activities. She left friends behind in California, but in Ashland she is closer to family and has worked hard to make new friends.

Her space needs have changed as well. She no longer feels the need to live in a house, but before her recent move to an apartment, she reevaluated the importance of the size of her living space.

Many of you, like Liz, may make multiple moves in your lifetime to satisfy your changing needs for place and space. Others, particularly those committed to living in a place you like, may want to explore the benefits of "universal design" principles if you build or remodel your home.

👁 Universal design principles are guidelines for house design that help ensure your home will be safe and comfortable for all ages. Including accessibility features such as a bedroom and bathroom space on the first floor, may make it possible for you to "age in place"—stay in the same home for many years.

 Your Savvy Sisters' Advice

- Identify your criteria for a new place to live. This will make your search process easier.

- Rent first when trying out a new location. Don't rush into a long-term housing commitment.

- Try out a new location at different seasons of the year.

- Identify your needs for space. First try to reorganize your current space to meet your needs.

- Do an audit of your current living space to determine its good and bad points for the future.

- Consider including universal design principles in your building or remodeling plans to accommodate changing physical needs as you age.

- Remember, you may have several more moves in your lifetime.

Reasons to Stay and Reasons to Move

After 50 increased job freedom or reduced family obligations creates more options for where you might live. You may want to propose to your employer that you work from home. Or, you may want to be self-employed and be able to work from anywhere. You may prefer hot and humid weather to a colder climate. The proximity of friends, family, or health care facilities may be important to you. If you have a spouse or partner, remember he or she may not always agree with your criteria for evaluating location or space needs. You'll need to consult each other to reach a consensus, a solution that meets both of your needs.

Sharing Space

Couples and others who share living space may find their needs don't change in tandem. One of the space issues that couples often encounter is the desire for individual, private space. One partner may start working from home or want a place for projects as their interests change. You may want your own tools such as telephone lines, computers, shop or kitchen gear, but you may have to share. Often, there is simply a need, psychological or emotional, for your own room or your own tools. These are issues that need to be negotiated. We'll talk more about couples' issues in Chapter 13 and help you anticipate your needs in the exercises below.

Place Needs Inventory

While the future is hard to predict, it's important to identify what's important to you when choosing a place to live. These criteria will help you decide whether to stay put or consider looking for a new place to live. Use the worksheet below to identify your place needs.

Criteria for Evaluating Place	Details: What are you looking for?	Rate 1 to 10; 10 = Very Important
Lifestyle		
Cost of living, taxes		
Educational interests		
Recreational interests		
Cultural interests		
Opportunities for paid work		
Opportunities for volunteer work		
Climate and landscape		
Friends and family nearby		
Health care availability		
Public transportation: airport, train, bus		
Low crime rate		
Familiarity with the community		

Now circle those items you rated "6" or higher. These are your *most important needs*. Ask your partner to do the same thing, independently. Compare the results and discuss them. Try to reach a consensus, a solution that meets both of your needs.

Space Needs Quiz

Ask yourself these questions about your present and future needs for space.

- Is my present living space too large, too small, or just right?

- Where (specific rooms, garden, deck, garage, workroom, other) do I currently spend most of my time? Will I need or want this same space in the future?

- What rooms are rarely used? Do I really need them? Will I need or want them in the future?

- What space do I wish I had? How would I use it?

- Could some rooms be used for more than one purpose? If so, what?

- What about outside space? Do I want a deck? Do I want a lawn or a garden? If so, will I take care of them, or will I hire someone to do it?

Ask your partner to answer these questions independently. Compare your results and discuss them.

> ❗
> ◉ Some daydreaming plus an honest assessment of your current location and space needs are the first steps in determining if you really want to move.

Resources to Help You with Your Place and Space Needs

Books

Berkus, Nate. *Home Rules: Transform the Place You Live into a Place You'll Love*. New York: Hyperion, 2005.

Bland, Warren R. *Retire in Style: 50 Affordable Places Across America*. Chester, NJ: Next Decade, 2002.

Faller, Bernard and Faller, Rhoda. *Moving the Nest: A Mid-Life Guide to Relocating*. Warrenton, VA: E. M. Press, 2001.

Morrow, Ed; Bykofsky, Sheree; & Rosenkranz, Rita. *Put Your House on a Diet: Declutter Your Home and Reclaim Your Life*. Emmaus, PA: Rodale, 2005.

Susanka, Sarah. *Creating the Not So Big House*. Newtown, CT: Taunton Press, 2001

Miscellaneous

The Chamber of Commerce in most towns will provide information on the weather, housing, economy, and leisure activities in their area. Also, many have websites.

Websites

Guidelines on creating accessible homes using universal design principles.

* http://www.aarp.org/families/home_design/
* www.aarp.org/universalhome/checklist.html
* www.oznet.ksu.edu/library/HOUS2/MF2213.pdf

5

Reality Strikes
The Illness and Loss Trigger

*Do we not all spend the greater part of our lives under
the shadow of an event that has not yet come to pass?*
Maurice Maeterlinck

Serious illness, whether our own or that of a close
friend or loved one, is the ultimate trigger for confronting
mortality. Even hearing of the death of a public figure or
someone we hardly knew may cause us to take stock of
our lives and choose to make the most of the rest of it.

Planning for the unexpected is a balancing act.
It requires that we live life to the fullest, while we
simultaneously accept the possibility of lost opportunities,
illness, and the prospect of death.

George Valliant in *Aging Well* describes a characteristic
of those who have serious health conditions but manage
to live fully: "They continue to live active lives while
taking care of themselves and sensibly living within their
limitations."

The following stories illustrate how illness and
loss altered the life choices of these individuals. Their

experiences point to steps you can take to prepare for the unexpected.

Unexpected Illness—Joe and Fern's Story

Joe and Fern did everything we advise in Chapters 2 and 4 about finance and location to create the life they wanted after 50. Joe identified the kind of work he wanted to do as a transition to retirement. Fern decided to stop working and devote herself to community service work. Joe says, "Our plan was to go into a community we thought we'd like to retire in and work from five to ten years, get to know the community well, and then make the decision whether that's where we'd settle down." They settled on Aiken, South Carolina, and launched the next phase of their life.

Then, the unexpected happened. Joe was diagnosed with prostate cancer. He had surgery and, fortunately, is now doing well. Joe is an active, positive man who describes himself as a cancer survivor. He is quick to report that his PSA (prostate specific antigen) score is now 0. But Fern, who worked in hospitals during her career and is used to illness, knows Joe is not always positive. "I think Joe's prostate cancer really shocked him," Fern says. "Every time we do a PSA test there is that dread, that fear." Even though there is a history of cancer in Joe's family, he didn't think it would happen to him.

The cancer caused Joe to rethink his work life—again. He decided to retire and spend more time with his family, particularly his "grandbabies." He and Fern had planned to volunteer for their church in a foreign country, but now Joe wants to be part of their grandchildren's growing up. "They pulled us right back in," he says, "I'm Daddy Joe to four of them."

Fern is philosophical about the direction their lives have taken. "You know you don't live forever," she says, "and we have reminders along the way."

Lessons from Joe and Fern

When we asked people who were retired what was important to them, they consistently talked about the need for financial security and good health. Joe and Fern were good planners, but they didn't anticipate the possibility of serious health problems when they planned to volunteer in a foreign country. And, although they had health insurance, their experience is a reminder to the rest of us to include the cost of health and long-term care insurance in our financial plans.

> **!**
> ◉ It's important to be receptive to a "Plan B" in life—when one door shuts another can be opened. This requires practicing healthy attitudes, maintaining appearance and fitness, having a wide range of interests, and continuing to develop your life skills.

Making a Plan After Loss—Taylor's Story

At 55, Taylor is concerned about what she calls "old, old age." For more than a decade Taylor has suffered from chronic fatigue syndrome (CFS). CFS caused Taylor to alter her career choices and to experience periodic depression and loss of stamina—issues Taylor believes are more commonly experienced by people in their 60s than in their 40s. Her life situation has also been affected by the illness and the likelihood of an imminent death of her mother.

Because she is more aware of aging than her contemporaries, and she worries about being alone in old age, Taylor is planning her life. Part of the plan she wrestles with is where she wants to live when she reaches "old, old age." She currently lives on the West Coast, but she's not sure where she'll end up—maybe back East. "I'll do some exploring," she says. "I'll drive around until I find someplace that feels good, a small town. I'll know it when I see it. I don't know yet. I've got too much to think about right now with a sick and dying mother."

Lessons from Taylor

Taylor wants to secure her own old age while at the same time she's struggling with the impending loss of her mother, a loss of vitality, and the loss of opportunities in her life caused by CFS. She knows she needs to put a plan together for herself. She also knows she will need to regroup after her mother's death and gain some perspective. Before she's ready to plan further, Taylor may need to take "a walk in the woods," a period of reflection during which she will give herself the freedom and time to decide what's important to her.

> ❗
> 👁 For those in the "sandwich generation"—those in midlife who are responsible for their children as well as one or both of their parents—it can be even tougher. They must plan to juggle their time, money, and energy in order to attend to both their families' and their own life issues.

The Shadow of Alzheimer's—Valerie's Story

Momentary forgetfulness is often called a "senior moment," a phrase popular with over-scheduled, highly stressed baby boomers. It signifies uneasiness with moments of memory loss. We ask ourselves, "Did I just forget, or is this the onset of something serious—maybe Alzheimer's?" While many of the people we interviewed for this book were in their 50s, a few older participants, like Valerie who is 80, can give us some perspective on our worries.

Valerie smiles easily and often. She loves a joke. "If I kid my grandchildren—if something will take eight years to finish, and I say, 'I won't be around for that,'—they say, 'Oh, Grandma, don't talk like that.' I tell them, 'at my age, I don't buy green bananas.'"

In spite of her jokes, Valerie is far too busy planning her next trip to dwell on illness and death. Yet, she admits that while the prospect of illness, particularly Alzheimer's, doesn't weigh on her mind, she can't help but think about it. "My step-mother, who was beautiful and outgoing, got Alzheimer's. It was terrible. I went through all the phases of seeing a loved one decline." Then, with a customary twinkle in her eye, she adds, "When I see my [baby boomer] daughter forgetting things, it makes me feel good. I know it's not just someone getting older who forgets."

Lessons from Valerie

Relax; everyone forgets things from time to time. Valerie has learned to balance reality with humor and distinguish between an occasional memory lapse, "a senior moment," and something more serious.

Currently, Alzheimer's and other forms of dementia afflict only a small percentage of those over 65. The possibility of dementia rises with age, however. Because of the population bubble of baby boomers turning 65 starting in 2011, researchers predict an Alzheimer's epidemic in coming years if a cure isn't found. Support Alzheimer's research.

Memory Boosters

There is much that can be done at any age to maintain and enhance memory. These tips from the Andrus Foundation and the Dana Alliance for Brain Initiatives may help keep your memory sharp. Check any ideas that you want to start practicing.

✔	Memory Boosters
	Relax—stress may cause memory lapses.
	Concentrate—pay attention to remember something later.
	Focus—reduce distraction.
	Slow down—rushing interferes with paying attention.
	Organize—keep important items in a designated place.
	Write it down—record important things when you first hear them.
	Repeat it—repetition improves recall. Use for names and new ideas.
	Visualize it—associate an image with something you hope to recall.

Your Savvy Sisters' Advice

Some of your Savvy Sisters' advice is such common sense that we blush to list it, but we will:

- Take your health and fitness seriously, and, if you are ill, don't organize your life around your illness.
- Organize your life around health-promoting activities.
- Keep your brain active through lifelong learning, training, travel, work, stimulating daily activities, and supportive relationships with other people.

- Reach out for support to friends, clergy, a grief support group, or a counselor if a loved one is seriously ill or dies.
- Be patient. The acceptance of loss and the expression of grief is a process that takes time.

The prospect of loss, death, and grief are inescapable, but they needn't become obsessions. The lesson they teach us is that life is fragile, and we must make the most of it.

Resources to Help You Prepare for the Unexpected

Books

Didion, Joan. *The Year of Magical Thinking.* New York: Alfred A. Knopf, 2005.

Doka, Kenneth J. and Davidson, Joyce D. *Caregiving and Loss: Family Needs, Professional Responses.* Washington, D.C.: Hospice Foundation of American, 2001.

Levang, Elizabeth. *When Men Grieve: Why Men Grieve Differently and How You Can Help.* Minneapolis: Fairview Press, 1998.

Shenk, D. *The Forgetting: Alzheimer's, Portrait of an Epidemic.* New York: Doubleday, 2001.

Websites

- www.alz.org
  Alzheimer's Association provides information, research, and resources.
- www.americanheart.org
  American Heart Association for information on heart disease.
- www.breastcancer.org
  Information and support for breast cancer patients.

- www.cancer.gov
  National Cancer Institute for information on cancer research.
- www.cancer.org
  American Cancer Society for information on cancer research.
- www.cdc.gov
  Center for Disease Control and Prevention.
- www.dana.org
  The Dana Alliance for Brain Initiatives provides information about brain research.
- www.health.harvard.edu
  Harvard Medical School gives advice and information on medical conditions, mental health, wellness and prevention.
- www.healthandage.com
  Interactive health information for people as they move towards their senior years.
- www.mayoclinic.com
  The Mayo Clinic provides resources for living well and managing a condition.
- www.prostate-cancer.org/
  For information on prostate cancer.

Part Three

Transitions Between Triggers and Plans

Triggers

In Part Two, we identified *triggers* as:

• Typical life events

• Life-altering experiences

• Insights

Triggers cause us to reconsider our lives.

The people we interviewed for this book talked most about these triggers: declining work satisfaction, concerns about financial security, changes in appearance and health, options for location and living space, and serious illness or loss. We talked about those topics in Chapters 1 through 5.

Transitions

For most of us there is a *transition* between a trigger experience and the actual planning for that phase.

The transition is a bridge between the end of one life phase and the beginning of the next. It's a time of reflection. It may be as brief as a Sunday afternoon walk in the woods or as extended as a trek in the Himalayas.

Trigger ➔ Reflection/Transition ➔ Plan

Bill Bridges in his book *Transitions: Making Sense of Life's Changes* describes a transition as a "neutral zone"—a time when a "new sense of self could gestate." A similar model developed by Kurt Lewin is used to describe change in organizations. Lewin uses an "ice cube" metaphor—unfreeze, change, and re-freeze—to suggest that there is an ending or letting go of old perspectives, a change or reflection process, and a pragmatic process of planning and setting new goals.

Many of the people we interviewed described a transition period of not knowing what they wanted to do next with their lives. In Chapter 5 on illness and loss, Taylor expected that when she was no longer caring for her mother, she would take time to find a new place to live. "I'll drive around until I find some place that feels good, a small town," she said. "I'll know it when I see it. I don't know yet." Taylor anticipated giving herself the gift of a transition period to think about what was important to her.

In the next two chapters, you'll learn some ways to make the transition successfully from one life phase to the next.

We've included a Midlife Values Inventory in the next chapter to help you determine if your life values are changing. And, because optimism is such an important personality trait of those people who thrive at midlife and beyond, in Chapter 7 we included some ideas about how thinking patterns can lead to an optimistic outlook during times of transition.

6

The Long Trek
The Transition Phase

You have to let go of an old thing
before you pick up a new one.
Bill Bridges

Our lives usually take a predictable course. Our adult
lives are set in motion during our 20s, 30s, and 40s. We go
to school and make job or career choices. Some of us marry
(perhaps more than once), and some of us start families
and work to provide for our children's education and well-
being. These are hectic, often sleep-deprived years. It's as
though a path has been rolled out for us, and we follow it.
We have little time for reflection.

By 50 we are approaching the end of a significant life
phase—what Gail Sheehy, whose book *Passages* was one
of the first popular studies of life phases, calls the "little
death of first adulthood."

As parents, we either no longer have day-to-day
responsibilities for our children, or we can imagine an
end to our more intense parenting.

In our work lives, most of us are either satisfied with our achievements or disappointed with our progress. Those of us who delayed or interrupted our careers may just now be ramping up to focus on work.

Even if we are satisfied with our progress, we may be bored. People in this life phase with whom we have done career coaching often tell us, "Financially, I need to work another ten or 15 years, but I don't want to keep doing the same thing. I want something more. The problem is I don't know what I want to do instead."

Midlife Crisis

For many people, coming to the end of this first "adulthood" provokes the trigger experiences we described in Part Two or the midlife crisis that Peggy Lee immortalized in her song "Is That All There Is?"

Harry Moody in *The Five Stages of the Soul* suggests that a midlife crisis is likely to be spiritual and involves a search for deeper meaning in life. And, although "midlife crisis" is what many people call this transition phase, Gene Cohen, author of *The Creative Age*, favors calling it the "reevaluation phase." Cohen believes that most adults in this phase benefit from reflecting on their lives.

> ❗ ◉ We need to allow ourselves a reflective transition between the closing of one life phase and the beginning of the next. And, if we attempt to plan for life after 50 without this transition, our planning may miss the mark.

The stories of Jane, Daniel, and Ruth provide examples of successful transitions.

The Long Trek, Life Without Structure—Jane's Story

Jane describes herself as a good girl who always got recognition through her job. Then, at 50, she took a trip to Nepal and embarked on a two-month trek in the Himalayas. The journey was the first time in her busy life that she experienced prolonged periods of silence.

"If asked before then what spiritual meant, I couldn't have defined it," she says. "Now I think it was a spiritual experience to be that close to myself and [to] realize the richness of the present."

The trek was the beginning of a transformation for Jane. When she returned, she found that she "appreciated quiet time and finally began hearing my own [inner] voice." She hadn't known herself as creative or spiritual, but now she started to see herself that way. She was interested in Buddhism prior to the trip, and after returning she began to meditate. "This led me to think about life without structure," Jane says.

The trek also led Jane to request a yearlong leave of absence from her work, and, at 55, Jane had a second opportunity to explore her life. During the year preparing for the leave, she was anxious and questioned herself: "Do I deserve it? Will I be productive? What does productive mean to me now?"

The journal she kept during this period reflected her anxiety. She worried about what other people would think of her. Her self-worth had been based on the recognition she received from others for her work achievements. She questioned whether she was still a valuable person if she wasn't producing praiseworthy work.

She says, "During my leave, I did some gardening, a little travel—not what people expected." Ultimately, her year off "opened space" for Jane to realize that to be a worthy person she didn't need to produce in the same ways

she always had. She opted for early retirement, and—
without anxiety—she's now enjoying life without the
structure of work.

Lessons from Jane

Jane and Susan, whom you met in Chapter 1 on work,
feared that if life were not filled with affirming work,
they'd lose their identities as competent professionals.
They'd be left not knowing who they were. Both women
needed time and psychological space to locate and listen
to their inner voice and to be guided by its wisdom. Jane
took the time over several years to find and listen to the
inner voice that helped her redefine her self-worth.

> **!**
> ◉ If life is not filled with the buzz and hum of work,
> there may appear to be a hole, an empty space. This
> empty space may be quickly filled with other activities,
> or it may be embraced and explored. The empty space is
> an invitation to listen to your self, to become reacquainted
> with the quiet, small voice crowded out by years of
> activity.

Serial Transitions—Daniel's Story

Daniel's transition began at 45 with a separation from
his wife, which included therapy. His therapist told him,
"Your life is on hold because of the uncertainty in your
marriage. Think about what you really want."

Daniel attended a Jesuit retreat and met a priest,
a Jungian psychologist, who suggested, "Get out of your
head and into your body." Daniel learned yoga, Rolfing,
Tai Chi and took a massage course. But, at first, he
"didn't know what to do with it all." He didn't know how
to integrate the bodywork into his life.

During this period a series of events were taking place. He was caring for his elderly parents—his father had Alzheimer's—and Daniel's job with the U.S. Public Health Service was "driving him nuts." So, he started planning for early retirement at 55. To prepare himself for another career, he completed a three-year occupational therapy program.

After years of trying to hold their marriage together, he and his wife divorced. By this time Daniel had retired and was a practicing occupational therapist; he had the flexibility to live where he chose. He prepared to sell the house that he and his wife had lived in for a number of years. While he was still trying to make sense of his divorce, he was also becoming integrated into the community as a single man and starting to date. He believed that if he didn't move quickly, however, he'd get too comfortable, settle in, and stop growing.

After his father died, his mother wanted to move to a residential community, so Daniel sold his house and bought his mother's condo in another town. The move and the proceeds from the sale of his house allowed Daniel to take a couple years off to pursue his interests.

Daniel's last 15 years have been marked with a series of life-changing events, each with its own transition. Over time he says he learned to use Jungian psychology, his Catholic spiritual life—in particular, *Contemplative Prayer* by Thomas Merton—and the bodywork to help him to understand himself better and to guide his journey through these transitions.

These days, he strives to create balance in his life. He recently met a woman who lives in Alaska and with whom he shares similar interests. This is the first serious relationship he's developed since his divorce. For now, they're traveling back and forth between California and Alaska to spend time together.

Lessons from Daniel

Daniel went through several transitions. He experimented with various intellectual, spiritual, and physical approaches to help him gain perspective. This has been a process of "reflecting in place," which may be more feasible for many of us than taking an actual trek.

> ❗
> 👁 People who have focused on the mental demands of their careers may need to learn to listen with both their heads and their hearts at midlife.

Some people describe listening as a spiritual experience; it may be religious or it may involve a deeper appreciation and understanding of family, love, nature, beauty, the environment, or a higher power. Others have found that some form of bodywork such as yoga or Tai Chi provides both physical and spiritual benefits.

A Transition from Death to the Next Phase of Life—Ruth's Story

When Wayne was nearing the end of his life, his wife, Ruth, checked Wayne out of the hospital and took him home for three weeks. "Everybody was against me, my children, everyone," Ruth says. But, it was a peaceful time. "It was wonderful. It made up for the dark days when he was irascible."

Immediately after Wayne's death, Ruth was exhausted and spent most of her time sleeping. Friends tried to reassure her that eventually she'd be ready to step back into her former life. They told her, "Oh, Ruth, you'll come back and lead this or that committee; you're good at it." But she felt it was time for others to assume those roles. Instead, Ruth joined the Renaissance Society at a local

University of California campus. She joined a singing group and enrolled in a writers' seminar.

Ruth now spends long hours writing at her computer. "It's just pouring out of me," she says, "mostly vignettes. They're usually humorous because I like to laugh. This is such fun. It surprises me because it just came upon me. I hadn't planned it. I'm writing poetry, too. I sent a minister friend a poem about Wayne's and my view of death. He said it was good. That just tickles me. I don't publish; I *distribute*. My Xerox bill is big."

Lessons from Ruth

In spite of opposition, Ruth chose to do what she intuitively felt was best: She cared for her husband at the end of his life. Then she used her newly discovered creativity to "take a walk in the woods"—a period of reflection to transcend the grief that followed his death. Ruth wrote the poem "Validation" several months after Wayne's death. The poem illustrates Ruth's use of poetry as a vehicle for understanding her transition from one life phase to the next. You'll find her poem in Resources.

> **!**
> ◉ Some people find that meditation, creative writing, or keeping a journal helps them gain clarity during a transition. Through these activities they quiet the chatter of their minds and listen to their inner voices.

The Need for Reflection

Described as one of the more influential writers on the psychology of middle age, Carl Jung suggested that a growing concern with one's inner self is a normal part of midlife. It was Jung's belief that while self-concern in a young person might be seen as unhealthy, for a person in midlife, "it is a duty and a necessity to devote serious attention to [one's] self."

The transitions for Jane, Daniel, and Ruth involved devoting serious attention to themselves. Jane managed to clear a psychological space in order to get reacquainted with her inner voice, Daniel gained insight through spiritual and physical exploration, and Ruth found healing self-expression through writing.

Each of these individuals navigated a midlife transition by turning inward. They set aside time for reflection and listened to their inner voices. They also reassessed their personal values. They discovered that their attitudes toward their work, life, and self-identity were shifting.

 Your Savvy Sisters' Advice

Find a method of personal reflection that suits you and helps you to explore your self-identity. Here are some ideas:

- Get back to nature: Walk, hike, bike, take up gardening.
- Keep a journal.
- Learn to meditate.
- Try your hand at writing, painting, or some other form of self-expression. Remember, this is for *you*. You don't have to share it with anyone, unless you want to.
- Read poetry.
- Go on a retreat.
- Wander a bit—take your time on a driving trip.

Reassess Your Values

There are many ways of describing the qualities, activities, or states of being that motivate, guide, and

direct our adult lives. The shorthand term for this is *values*.
We have found that the values most important to adults
tend to cluster into six core categories:

- Achievement and Work
- Creativity
- Love and Intimacy
- Self-actualization
- Self-identity
- Service

We've also found that the values that were important
to us at 30 or 40 may not be as important to us at 50 or 60.
The values that take center stage change, depending on
the phase of our lives. Sometimes, this value shift occurs
without our conscious awareness and creates the emotional
flatness that some experience as a midlife crisis. Becoming
consciously aware of these value shifts can be a trigger
event.

exercise►

Midlife Values Inventory

Reassess your values by completing the following
Midlife Values Inventory. The results will help you
determine what is most important to you now.

1. From the 52 values listed, pick the ten that are *most*
   important to you now. Don't rank order them, just
   put a "✓" in the Important column.

2. Next to the ten values you picked, indicate to what
   extent your behavior demonstrates that you live
   those values now. Show this by giving each of the
   ten a rating (in the Rating column) from 1 to 10.

   1 = No one would know this is important to me.

   10 = My behavior demonstrates this is very important to me.

Midlife Values Inventory

Values	Important	Rating	Values	Important	Rating
Achievement/Work			Family happiness		
Advancement			Friendship		
Adventure			Love		
Authority			Nurturing		
Challenge			Parenting		
Competitiveness			Social networks		
Fame			**Self-actualization**		
Financial security			Fulfillment		
Goals			Inner peace		
Intellectual stimulation			Integrity		
Interpersonal competence			Justice		
Leadership			Order		
Problem solving			Personal development		
Power			Spirituality		
Prestige			Wisdom		
Recognition			**Self-identity**		
Results			Autonomy		
Technical competence			Confidence		
Winning			Health		
Creativity			Independence		
Creating something new			Self-esteem		
Fun			Self-reliance		
Humor			Security		
Joy			Structure		
Passion			Service		
Play			Caretaking		
Love/Intimacy			Compassion		
Affection			Making a difference		
Belonging			Mentoring		

3. Did you discover that some values are more important to you now than they used to be? What does this tell you?

4. Did you find that you checked a value as important to you, but you are not currently living your life in tune with that value? (This may mean that your values have shifted away from what was important to you in the past. Or, it may mean that it's time to rethink your priorities.) What do these results mean to you?

Taking time for reflection at midlife helps ensure that the plans we make for the next phase of our lives satisfy our changing values and priorities and the stirrings of our soul.

Resources to Help You Navigate from One Life Phase to the Next

Books

Bridges, William. *Transitions: Making Sense of Life's Changes*. Reading, MA: Addison-Wesley, 1980.

Brim, Gilbert. Ambition: *How We Manage Success and Failure Throughout our Lives*. New York: Basic Books, 1992.

Chirboga, D. A. "Mental Health at the Midpoint: Crisis, Challenge, or Relief?" in *Midlife Myths*. Eds. S. Hunter and M. Sundel. Newbury Park, CA: Sage Publications, 1989.

Cohen, Gene D. *The Creative Age: Awakening Human Potential in the Second Half of Life*. New York: Harper Collins, 2000.

Fischer, Norman. *Taking Our Places: The Buddhist Path to Truly Growing Up*. San Francisco: Harper Collins, 2003.

Hudson, Frederic M. *The Adult Years Mastering the Art of Self-Renewal*. San Francisco: Jossey-Bass, 1991.

Hultgren, Ruth. *Looking Into the Rearview Mirror*. Bloomington, IN: 1st Books Library, 2003.

Jeffers, Susan. *Feel the Fear and Do It Anyway*. New York: Ballantine Books, 1987.

Jung, C. G. "The Stages of Life," in *Collected Works: Vol. 8. The Structure and Dynamics of the Psyche*. New York: Pantheon, 1960.

Moody, Harry R. and Carroll, David. *The Five Stages of the Soul*. New York: Anchor Books, 1997.

Progoff, Ira. *At a Journal Workshop*. New York: Jeremy P. Tarcher/Putnam, 1992.

(Also check out www.intensivejournal.org for journal workshops in your area.)

Sheehy, Gail. *New Passages: Mapping Your Life Across Time*. New York: Ballantine Books, 1996.

Sheehy, Gail. *Sex and the Seasoned Woman Pursuing the Passionate Life*. New York: Random House, 2006.

Thornton, Mark. *Meditation in a New York Minute*. Boulder, CO: Sounds True, 2004.

Young-Elsendrath, P. *The Resilient Spirit: Transforming Suffering into Meaning and Purpose*. Reading, MA: Perseus Books, 1996.

Miscellaneous

"Validation"

Dear Friend, I wanted you to know,
covered six months by mountain snow;
there is no doubt in our shared belief
that death is just the old brown leaf
required to fall.

For new green leaves need space to sprout
unhampered by the lingering clout
of dying leaves, whose heavy hold
takes space from all the young and bold
who must appear.

A sense of green in darkened boughs
increases daily 'round the house;
crabapple blossoms show pink, then white,
a dazzling scene after months of night
which had to end.

(Reprinted from *Looking Into the Rearview Mirror* with permission of Ruth Hultgren)

What does "productive" mean to me now?

From Jane's story

7

She Had High Hopes
The Benefits of Optimism

A merry heart doeth good like a medicine,
but a broken spirit drieth the bones.
Proverbs 17:22

Have you noticed that some people seem to navigate smoothly through life's transitions while others are routinely beached on a rocky shore? The difference may be attributed to optimism. Optimists are resilient and have positive expectations for themselves in spite of periodic setbacks. When faced with uncertainty, they choose the option that provides personal growth. Other people get bogged down in fear or pessimism.

But take heart, pessimists—it's possible to *learn* to be more optimistic! Optimism is such an important quality when facing a transition or planning for midlife, we believe it deserves its own chapter.

A long-term study of five freshmen classes from Harvard, documented by George Valliant in *Aging Well*, showed that, in general, optimists are healthier than pessimists, and they may even live longer. Valliant found the *habit* of optimistic thinking was apparent in the study's participants in their 20s and continued to benefit them throughout their lives.

Similar results were described by the epidemiologist and author, David Snowdon, in *Aging With Grace: What the Nun Study Teaches Us About Leading Longer, Healthier, and More Meaningful Lives.* An examination of the autobiographies of 179 Catholic nuns, written when they were around 22 years old, revealed that positive emotional content predicted who would live the longest.

Although scientists don't yet clearly understand the physiological and lifestyle link between optimism and long life, it's clear there is one.

Learning to be Optimistic

It's fair to say that even staunch optimists aren't optimistic all the time. Some people carry pessimistic, as well as optimistic, thinking patterns from their childhood. It's also possible that in certain situations, a bit of pessimism may provide a useful reality check.

Martin Seligman, author of *Learned Optimism*, claims optimism can be learned at any age. Seligman suggests there are thinking patterns associated with optimism that enhance health and achievement and minimize depression. For example, one such thinking pattern is one's explanatory style—"your habitual way of explaining events." Optimists believe that the cause of negative events is temporary, and the cause of positive events is permanent and within their control.

Becky's story illustrates an optimistic explanatory style that helps her move through a transition.

Choosing Optimism—Becky's Story

Although Becky is 48, today she thinks of herself as 50. Her blond hair has new silver streaks. When she was 40 and looked in the mirror, she liked what she saw:

a sexual and sensual woman with the power to attract men. Now she sees loose skin she isn't sure is "fixable" at the gym. She feels she has lost her power to attract, and she grieves that loss.

In the past, mothering gave Becky's life meaning. But her daughter is in college now, and her son will soon graduate from high school. Sometimes she wonders if she has been too good a mother. When they were growing up, she told her kids they could have or be anything in life they wanted. Now she suspects she will lose them to the world, and she doesn't know where that will leave her. What will her role be now? What will give meaning to her life? She thinks, "Maybe I should be *doing* something—get a job," but she doesn't know what she wants to do.

Lately, she has begun to feel boring. She's not bored; she has plenty to do, but she feels as though she's a boring person. Death has been on her mind, too. She has never feared death, but now she's sharply aware of her own mortality. Becky describes her mental state as "emptiness," and she's eager to feel passion in her life again.

Becky explained that she has experienced junctures before when she felt dried up and just wanted to spend her time watching old movies. So she knows these "rough patches" are temporary. She thinks she should examine her belief systems now, particularly her beliefs about the value of work and income. Her "explanatory style," what she tells herself about her life, is to habitually think of herself as a resilient person. She believes her current feelings are temporary, and if she's patient and lives with the discomfort for a while, "something will come in." In her heart, Becky knows this is an uncomfortable but important life phase.

Lessons from Becky

To hear Becky's story one might think she's pessimistic and depressed, but she isn't. Her experiences with similar phases allow her to be hopeful. As is common for optimists, Becky is confident the emptiness she feels will give way to renewed passion and clarity in her life—it always has before.

❗ ◉ It's the rare person who never has a rough patch in his or her life. Most of us have times when we're down. The issue is not the down times; the issue is what you *tell* yourself about those times. You can allow yourself to become overwhelmed by negativity and pessimism, or you can tell yourself "this too shall pass" and anticipate returning to a more optimistic frame of mind.

Optimism vs. Pessimism

Compared to optimists, pessimists tend to see negative events as permanent, universal, and beyond their control. Linda, whom you met in Chapter 2 on financial security, is such a person.

Linda fears she'll become a bag lady. She's afraid of living past the time she can take care of herself financially. She's afraid of the unknown, and, for Linda, her eventual retirement is "the big unknown." There seem to be no positive role models in Linda's life. "My sister ended up poor," she says, "with health problems and always negative. I see her living on the edge, and I know I never want to be in that position." In spite of her wish to live life differently than her sister, Linda seems helpless to change her situation now or in the future. She is pessimistic, fearful, and has not yet taken action to put a plan in place for her life after 50.

Thinking Patterns

Martin Seligman calls people who mull over bad events, "ruminators." He believes the thinking patterns of pessimism, coupled with rumination, put people at risk for depression. Changing either rumination or pessimism relieves depression and helps people feel more optimistic. Louise is the oldest person we interviewed, and we think she has a lot to teach us about changing our thinking patterns, nurturing optimism, and living life after 50.

Letting Go of Worry—Louise's Story

At 93 Louise is healthy, lives alone, and is fiercely independent. We met her when she was attending her 41st Elderhostel workshop.

We asked her how she makes decisions about her life. She credits the Serenity Prayer (see Resources). "I make a decision and go forward," she said. "There's nothing I can do about what's happened. If something isn't the way I want it and I can change it, then I do something to change it. If I can't change it, I either accept living with it or walk away." Once she developed that philosophy in her 50s, she stopped mentally "eating my guts out" and put an end to 20 years of chronic ulcerative colitis. "It just struck me like a bolt of lightening. You can't change another person or situation; you can only change yourself. Once I really internalized that, it wasn't just a motto on the wall, it was a turning point."

Lessons from Louise

When Louise stopped ruminating about people and events she was helpless to change, her mental and physical health improved. She began thinking like an optimist. When negative things happened that were within her power to control, she took action.

Louise changed the way she thought. The benefits of changing one's thinking patterns were born out by a longevity study conducted at Yale University. Their research demonstrated that those people who think positively about getting older live seven-and-one-half years longer than those who think negatively. This is a greater gain in longevity than that associated with maintaining low blood pressure, low cholesterol, a healthy weight, exercising regularly, or abstaining from smoking!

> **!**
> 👁 You can learn to be more optimistic. Optimism, positive expectations, and resiliency are important qualities during midlife transition. A positive approach to life will "fuel" you through periods of uncertainty and will give you mental stamina for making healthy choices for your future.

Your Savvy Sisters' Advice

- Learn to argue with your knee-jerk pessimistic responses.
- Monitor your habitual thinking processes. What you tell yourself about events (your explanatory style) affects how you feel about them.
- Identify those things in your life that you can control and those you can't. Make changes wherever you can to achieve your goals. Don't waste your physical and psychic energy on things you can't control.
- Distance yourself from negative people and events.
- Make it a habit to approach life with a positive point of view.

Assessing Your Positive Attitude

Perhaps you've never considered yourself to be an optimist, but now you're beginning to see the benefits of changing your thinking patterns. Start becoming an optimist by assessing your optimism quotient. Take the following quiz, courtesy of Dr. Wallace Schmidt, Professor of Communication at Rollins College, Winter Park, Florida.

Assess the degree to which you approach your life from a positive point of view.

	Assessing Your Positive Attitude (1 = Rarely and 5 = Almost Always)
1. I concentrate and focus on all the ways a thing might be done instead of focusing on the problems and obstacles.	1 2 3 4 5
2. I compliment and show appreciation to others whenever possible and avoid criticizing them.	1 2 3 4 5
3. I think about my strong points, my abilities, my personality, and reasons for self-worth.	1 2 3 4 5
4. The first thing I say to others, and have them say to me, is something good.	1 2 3 4 5
5. I surround myself with positive-minded people.	1 2 3 4 5
6. I cannot successfully wish away a down day; therefore I accept it as it is, for it will pass.	1 2 3 4 5
7. I look forward to learning something new every day and embark on major new projects regularly.	1 2 3 4 5
8. I always look for and expect the best in people, knowing that even if I am occasionally disappointed, we both still benefit.	1 2 3 4 5
9. I tell myself that others can stop me temporarily, but only I can stop myself on a permanent basis.	1 2 3 4 5

Positive Attitude Assessment (continued)

	Assessing Your Positive Attitude (1 = Rarely and 5 = Almost Always)				
10. I tell myself that when I blame others, I am getting further away from improving things for myself.	1	2	3	4	5
11. I tell myself that the biggest risk in life is avoiding risks.	1	2	3	4	5
12. I take regular, positive steps to eliminate worry about problems that I have some control over and can change for the better.	1	2	3	4	5
13. I get regular exercise and rest to maintain my positive attitude, efficiency, and energy.	1	2	3	4	5
14. I walk briskly, sit upright, relax, and breathe deeply.	1	2	3	4	5
15. I use positive body language to influence myself— I smile.	1	2	3	4	5
16. I periodically make a list of all the positive things I've done in my life and how I did them.	1	2	3	4	5
17. I truly believe that good things should, can, and will happen to me.	1	2	3	4	5
18. I strive NOT to see difficulties in every opportunity, but opportunities in every difficulty.	1	2	3	4	5
19. I set small goals that I'm 90 percent certain of achieving, and as I reach these goals, I set new and larger ones.	1	2	3	4	5
20. I tell myself that to make no decision is often a bad decision.	1	2	3	4	5

Add the values of the numbers you circled.
If your score is:

- 90-100—It's possible you're too optimistic; make sure you're optimism is grounded in reality.
- 80-90—Solidly optimistic.
- 60-80—Optimistic more often than not.
- 40-60—Pessimistic more often than not.

Use the items on the quiz as a guide for thinking and acting as an optimist. Acquiring an optimistic point of view offers profound physical and mental benefits.

Resources for Learning More About Optimism

Books

Beck, Martha. *Finding Your Own North Star*. New York: Three Rivers Press, 2001.

Gilbert, Daniel. *Stumbling on Happiness*. New York: Knopf, 2006.

Layard, Richard. *Happiness Lessons from a New Science*. New York: Penguin Press, 2005.

Ricard, Matthieu. *Happiness: A Guide to Developing Life's Most Important Skill*. London: Little Brown & Co., 2007.

Sadler, William. *The Third Age: 6 Principles of Growth and Renewal After Forty*. Cambridge, MA: Perseus Books, 2000.

Seibert, Al. *The Resiliency Advantage*. San Francisco: Berrett-Koehler Publishers, Inc., 2005.

Seligman, Martin. *Learned Optimism: How to Change Your Mind and Your Life*. New York: Pocket Books, 1990. (Includes a section with specific skills for changing your thinking patterns from pessimism to optimism.)

Seligman, Martin. *Authentic Happiness: Using the New Positive Psychology to Realize Your Potential for Lasting Fulfillment*. New York: Free Press, 2002.

Snowdon, David. *Aging With Grace: What the Nun Study Teaches Us About Leading Longer, Healthier, and More Meaningful Lives*. New York: Bantam Books, 2001.

Valliant, George E., M.D. *Aging Well: Surprising Guideposts to a Happier Life from the Landmark Harvard Study of Adult Development.* Boston: Little Brown, 2002.

Website

- www.healthandage.com
  Ken and Mary Gergen's "Positive Aging Newsletter." Go to their website to subscribe.
- www.reflectivehappiness.com
  Martin Seligman's Authentic Happiness site.

Miscellaneous

The Serenity Prayer is attributed to Dr. Reinhold Neibuhr. The first stanza is widely quoted:

God grant me SERENITY to
accept the things I cannot change;
COURAGE to change the things I can;
and WISDOM to know the difference.

Part Four

What Will I Do With My Time?

Your Savvy Sisters think it's safe to say that we all want our lives after 50 to be filled with purpose and passion. In Part Four, we will help you make choices about your interests in work, volunteering, creativity, learning, personal development, and travel. These are the activities that the people we interviewed told us were most important to them.

As you begin this process, the images and stereotypes imposed by the media about life after 50 may confuse you about your options and choices. Advertisements targeting people over 50 often show fit, active people living a life of leisure. Other images portray older adults mentally or physically declining, needing medication to get through life. It's easy to project an unrealistically youthful and ambitious lifestyle or one that's negative and depressing.

We may ask ourselves, "What are people in their 50s and 60s *supposed* to look and feel like, anyway? What can I do? Is there an *ideal* way to live my life after 50?" Your Savvy Sisters believe you must choose your own path based on your values, interests, finances, health, talents, and skills.

So, before you answer the question, "What will I do with my time?" you need a few more pieces of information. By completing the Midlife Transitions Inventory below you will identify your strengths, skills, and interests, as well as the activities you are drawn to, and those you want to avoid. This information and the chapters in this section will help you plan your time, activities, and goals for your next life phase.

exercise▸

Midlife Transitions Inventory

In the Midlife Transitions Inventory you will explore your work and life activities. Start with your current activities and retrace your life, by decade, back at least 25 years. You may wish to continue this process back to graduation from high school or college. If you've worked for the same employer for a long time, break your experience into chunks of time indicating your most significant assignments, titles, or roles.

You may want to complete this exercise yourself or ask your spouse, partner, or a friend to interview you. Record your answers on blank sheets of paper or in the spaces below.

Section A: Your History

1. Since 2000

a. What job(s), paid or unpaid, did you hold during this period? List your title(s) and employer(s):

b. What were the most important skills required?

c. What did you like/not like about your work during this period?

d. What are the most useful things you learned about yourself from work during this period?

e. What significant activities were you involved in with family, friends, or the community?

f. What are the most useful things you learned about yourself from these activities?

g. What learning activities, work or personal, were you involved in? Why did you choose those areas of learning?

h. What were your ambitions and long-range goals during this time period? Have you realized those ambitions or goals?

   i. What were the most significant decisions of your
          life during this period?

   j. What did you enjoy the most during this period?
          Be specific.

2. During the 1990s

   a. What job(s), paid or unpaid, did you hold during
          this period? List your title(s) and employer(s):

   b. What were the most important skills required?

   c. What did you like/not like about your work during
          this period?

   d. What are the most useful things you learned about
          yourself from work during this period?

   e. What significant activities were you involved in
          with family, friends, or the community?

   f. What are the most useful things you learned about
          yourself from these activities?

   g. What learning activities, work or personal, were
          you involved in? Why did you choose those areas
          of learning?

h. What were your ambitions and long-range goals during this time period? Have you realized those ambitions or goals?

i. What were the most significant decisions of your life during this period?

j. What did you enjoy the most during this period? Be specific.

3. During the 1980s

a. What job(s), paid or unpaid, did you hold during this period? List your title(s) and employer(s):

b. What were the most important skills required?

c. What did you like/not like about your work during this period?

d. What are the most useful things you learned about yourself from work during this period?

e. What significant activities were you involved in with family, friends, or the community?

f. What are the most useful things you learned about yourself from these activities?

g. What learning activities, work or personal, were you involved in? Why did you choose those areas of learning?

h. What were your ambitions and long-range goals during this time period? Have you realized those ambitions or goals?

i. What were the most significant decisions of your life during this period?

j. What did you enjoy the most during this period? Be specific.

Section B: Reflection

1. When and where do you feel fully alive and excited now? Under what conditions does this occur?

2. When and where does your life feel dull and routine now? What conditions produce that?

3. Do you sometimes have regrets? "If only I'd done ____." What do you wish you had done differently?

4. What are you really *good* at? What strengths and/or skills do you have to build on?

5. What do you do *poorly*? What do you want to develop or correct? What do you want to ignore or avoid?

6. What do you want to *stop* doing or do much less of?

7. What do you want to *start* doing or do much more of?

8. What do you want to learn or develop in yourself?

Section C: Themes and Common Factors

Review your answers by yourself and/or with your spouse, partner, or a friend.

- **Section A** deals with your past choices, decisions, experiences, and the skills and knowledge you acquired. What themes, trends, and/or common factors do you see in your answers?

- **Section B** is designed to help you think about the aspects of your life that you're best at and give you the greatest satisfaction. You may want to spend more time on them now and in the future. What themes, trends, and/or common factors do you see in your answers?

- What did you learn about yourself from the Midlife Transitions Inventory that will help with Your Life After 50 Plan?

What are people in their 50s and 60s
supposed to look and feel like, anyway? What can I do?
Is there an ideal way to live my life after 50?

Part Four

8

9 to 5
Rethinking Work

Life is a process of becoming, a combination of states
we have to go through. Where people fail is that
they wish to elect a state and remain in it.
Anais Nin

We are the first generation to express a strong desire to
work after traditional retirement age. Even if we aren't at
retirement age, we may want to rethink work. We may not
want to keep doing what we're doing now, or continue how
we're doing it, for the next 20 or 30 years. We may love our
work but want to reduce the hours we work, or we may
want to shift from "doing" to consulting or teaching. Others
may want to start new careers after 50.

According to an AARP study "Staying Ahead of the
Curve," a survey of 1,500 working Americans ages 45 to 74:

- 84 percent said they would work even if they were
  financially set for life.
- 76 percent said they enjoyed working.
- 70 percent are searching for better work/life balance.

- 69 percent said they plan to work after traditional retirement.

Why Work?

There are many reasons to work besides a paycheck. We may enjoy the social connections, thrive on the intellectual challenges, or need the sense of identity or self-esteem that work provides. Sometimes we have strong interests and drives that compel us to work. Morgan, Betsy, and Jacqui, whose stories follow, have rethought how and why they want to work after 50.

Financial Need—Morgan's Story

At age 52, Morgan, a trained physicist and manager, was looking at three more years before he could retire with full benefits. Then he unexpectedly lost his high-tech management job. He needed to continue earning money in order to support his lifestyle and prepare for retirement. So, he decided to parlay his experience in recruiting an educated, technical workforce into a consulting business.

Shortly after starting his business, he was asked by a local urban university to work part time as a liaison between industry and higher education. He accepted this job, and after a couple of years, he dropped his consulting business because he wanted better work/life balance. Part-time work provided enough money for him to feel financially secure, enjoy the sociability of the office, and pursue some of his hobbies. As he jokes, "I can't do it all plus fish!"

Morgan spent a lot of time thinking about what he wanted to do when he didn't have to work. He also thought about how he'd pay for it. He didn't want to get caught in the feeling of not having enough money, because he also had financial responsibilities for his mother and mother-in-law. He admitted that his problem was *not* being "tight with money."

After a successful part-time career in higher education, Morgan recently set a retirement date—ten years after he initially thought he'd retire. He says that if his finances had been different, he probably would have left work earlier. But he feels financially secure now, and he's looking forward to traveling and the hobbies (professional level woodworking and photography) he put on hold several years ago.

Lessons from Morgan

Morgan's transition to a university job was prompted by his financial needs. He analyzed his needs for the future, recognizing that he had family responsibilities as well as "champagne tastes." He chose part-time work because it gave him the opportunity for better work/life balance, financial security, and social interaction.

Intellectual Challenge and Social Drive—Betsy's Story

Betsy, 60, a human resources consultant from Massachusetts whom you met in Chapter 3 on appearance and fitness, shared her perspectives on work. "I love work. At this age I see and understand more than I used to. I want to help people." After she recently left her employer of 22 years, Betsy started a consulting business. She wanted to work for several more years and still be part of "the action." At this stage of her life she feels "more creative" than she did when she was younger.

During her 50s Betsy started to assess what she needed for personal growth. She completed a doctoral program, a decision she says was "one of the best decisions of my life." Prior to her work in this program, she didn't know what she stood for. Now, she feels more confident of her opinions. She has been able to clarify her own "voice."

Lessons from Betsy

Betsy's focus on personal growth in her early 50s established a sense of self on which to build in later years. She now understands her need for intellectual challenge and professional and social interaction, so she has chosen to continue working part time. Her advice for others is: "Clarify what you want to do, what really turns you on. Focus, but let things evolve, too. Revisit your choices continually."

Helping Others—Jacqui's Story

Jacqui got a late start on her career after graduating from college at 40. She knows she won't be ready to retire at a "normal" age, but she doesn't want to. Working beyond normal retirement age is important to her because she's had a shorter time to develop her career.

Jacqui is a self-employed marriage and family therapist who plans to work into her 70s. She provides counseling to low-income clients. She also sells products to enhance romance for couples such as books, furnishings for the home and garden, personal care items, and jewelry. An inner drive to help others motivated her to establish a business that represents her values. Her energies are directed toward growing her counseling center and developing materials to help people learn about love. She doesn't see her work ending at traditional retirement age because her work is a "crystallizing of my life."

Lessons from Jacqui

Jacqui recognizes that helping others is an important part of her life and provides her best option for future fulfillment. She knows that her work needs to represent her values and focus in specific areas.

Benefits of Work

Morgan continued working because of a financial need, but he found his work also satisfied a social need. Betsy enjoys the intellectual and social stimulation of work. Jacqui's need to help others gives her work meaning. They each knew they didn't want to stop working and eventually opted to transition from full- to part-time employment. They continue to reassess what they want and need from work.

> ❗ ◉ Work at midlife can offer benefits besides money and career advancement. Your work can be a renewed expression of your life-long search for meaning.

Why do you want to work? Are any of the following reasons motivators for you to work?

- Intellectual stimulation
- An enthusiastic interest or compelling drive
- An opportunity to be productive
- Social interaction
- Financial need
- Building a legacy
- A contribution to society

Workplace Realities for Older Workers

According to the U.S. Bureau of Labor Statistics more than 25 percent of the working population will have reached retirement age by the year 2010, leaving a potential worker shortage close to 10 million. As boomers start retiring, there'll be more jobs than workers to fill them. Visionary employers realize this shortage of workers is rapidly approaching. Some are developing policies focused on attracting and retaining older workers. These employers realize that older workers have a strong work ethic, offer invaluable experience, and can serve as mentors for younger employees.

Whether or not you work for a visionary employer, it's important to rethink what's really important to you about your work and then to assess your options. Ask yourself the question, "Am I living to work or working to live?" Your answer will affect how you plan your work life and the options you choose.

You've already done some thinking about your work if you completed the Midlife Transitions Inventory in Part Four. We'll come back to it. First, let's explore some options.

Part-time or Full-time Work

For many people, 50-60 hours is a normal workweek. But even a 40-hour week may be too long to maintain a good balance among work, family, and other interests. That is why some people consider the following options for part-time employment:

- Part-time, same employer
- Phased retirement—same employer, same benefits, fewer hours, earned income plus pension income
- Part-time, self-employed
- Part-time, working for someone else

Part-time work may be structured as:

- Intermittent work
- Contract work
- Job-sharing
- Flexible time
- Telecommuting

> ! ◉ Part-time work often allows us to be more productive, positive, and energetic. A shorter workweek gives employees an opportunity to rejuvenate themselves and explore other interests.

Health Issues

Some jobs involve physical or psychological demands that encourage or even force workers to retire. If that's your situation, you may need to assess your workload and determine what changes might be possible if you'd like to continue working. Adaptations might include switching to a less strenuous position, sharing a job with another worker, or adjusting your pace of work. Sometimes something as simple as an ergonomically correct workstation will make it possible for you to continue working.

Training

If you feel bored and want to take on new challenges, whether full or part time, think about pursuing the training opportunities your employer offers. If there are none appropriate for your interests, explore the offerings of your local community college or university.

Changing What You Do

We recommend four important steps if you're ready to rethink work:

1. Attitude adjustment
2. Examination of work and life values fit
3. Experimentation
4. Exploration

The next four sections provide exercises to help you rethink work.

Attitude Adjustment

As we discussed in Chapter 7, an optimistic attitude enhances achievement as well as health. You have a much better chance for successful change if you have a positive mental attitude toward a new work environment, view your own set of skills and abilities as assets, and if you are excited about the possibilities for the future. So, think positive! You may want to review the Assessing Your Positive Attitude exercise in Chapter 7.

Work and Life Values Fit

This next exercise will help you think about how to manage the transition from what you are currently doing to what you might do in the future. Be sure you have completed your Midlife Values Inventory in Chapter 6, and keep it handy. An example follows the instructions.

Instructions:

1. Think about a specific, typical *workday*. On a sheet of blank paper, jot down a list of all your activities from the time you got up until you went to bed.

2. Look at your Midlife Values Inventory and see how the events of your *workday* match with your *top ten values*. Jot down the values you associate with each of your activities. What conclusions do you draw from these results?

3. On a second sheet of blank paper, complete the same kind of list of activities for a typical *weekend* day.

4. Match your *top ten values* with your *weekend* activities. What conclusions do you draw from these results?

Example:

Typical Workday Activities	Associated Values
Breakfast with my family	Parenting, Affection
Rode to work with colleagues	Social networks
Led a team meeting	Interpersonal competence
Worked on a new design project	Technical competence
Met with my boss for review of work	Recognition
Helped train a new employee	Mentoring
Attended an aerobics class after work	Social networks, Fun, Health
Had dinner with my family	Parenting, Affection
Played cards with my spouse and son	Fun

Example:

Typical Weekend Activities	Associated Values
Attended my son's soccer game	Parenting, Social networks
Met (with my spouse) with a financial advisor	Financial security
Played tennis	Fun, Health
Went to a party	Social networks, Fun

exercise▸

Experimentation

Now, let's try a little experiment in which you will redesign your typical workday and weekend day. Be sure you have completed your Midlife Transitions Inventory in Part Four. Review your answers to Sections B and C before beginning this exercise.

Instructions:

1. Think about which activities you would eliminate and which you would keep or add if you could *redesign your workday*. On another blank sheet of paper write down a revised version of your workday, as you would *like* it to be.

2. Look at your Midlife Values Inventory and see how the events of your *redesigned workday* match with your *top ten values*. Jot down the values you associate with each of your activities. What conclusions do you draw from these results? What conclusions do you draw by comparing how your values are satisfied in your typical workday and in your redesigned workday?

3. If you are thinking of retiring, think about how you would like to spend a typical retirement day. On a blank sheet of paper write down the activities you would like to be involved in on a typical day (your weekend activity summary may give you some ideas).

4. Match your top ten values with each of these activities. Do you satisfy more or fewer of your values on a retirement day or a workday? What conclusions do you draw from these results?

Experimentation will help you think about many possibilities for change. Try out several designs. Once you have a plan you're comfortable with, we encourage you to move on to the next exercise.

Exploration

By this time you probably have some good ideas for rethinking work, or maybe you've decided retirement looks interesting. You're ready now to explore your ideas for new activities or changes to your current activities.

Record your answers to the following questions on a blank sheet of paper.

1. What activity(s) do you want to focus on?
2. Who do you know who shares your interests in these activities?
3. Who can you network with to find out more about these activities?
4. What courses related to these activities are available?
5. What organizations focus on your interests?
6. With whom can you discuss your ideas for changes at work?

The questions you've answered in these exercises should give you some ideas about what to do next.

Your Savvy Sisters' Advice

- Think about what motivates you to work now and what might motivate you in the future.
- Figure out what you can afford financially before you make any life changes.
- Share your thoughts with your partner, spouse, or a close friend.

- Keep in mind that positive change is possible for most people.
- Remember that small changes can sometimes have significant impact. You don't need to completely alter your lifestyle and work obligations to live a more satisfying life.
- Explore, explore, explore.

Resources to Help You Rethink Work

Books

Abrams, Rhonda. *What Business Should I Start? 7 Steps to Discovering the Ideal Business for You.* Palo Alto: The Planning Shop, 2004.

Attard, Janet. *The Home Office and Small Business Answer Book.* NewYork: Henry Holt, 2000.

Bolles, Richard. *The 2007 What Color is Your Parachute?* Berkeley, CA: Ten Speed Press, 2006. (Revised and updated yearly.)

Busse, Richard. *Fired, Laid Off or Forced Out: A Complete Guide to Severance Benefits and Your Rights When You're Starting Over.* Naperville, IL: Sourcebooks, 2005

DeLuca, Matthew. *How to Get a Job in 90 Days or Less: A Realistic Action Plan for Finding the Right Job Fast.* New York: McGraw-Hill, 1995.

Farr, Michael. *Overnight Career Choice: Discover Your Ideal Job in Just a Few Hours.* Indianapolis, IN: JIST Publishing, 2006.

Finnigan, Dan; Jones, Christopher and Karasu, Marc. *Your Next Move: Success Strategies for Midcareer Professionals.* New York: Sterling Publishing, 2006.

Hendricks, Mark. *Grow Your Own Business.* Irvine, CA: Entrepreneur Press, 2001.

Lesonsky, Rieva. *Start Your Own Business*. Irvine, CA: Entrepreneur Press, 2001.

Oliver, Vicky. *301 Smart Answers to Tough Interview Questions*. Naperville, IL: Sourcebooks, 2005.

Sedlar, Jeri and Miners, Rick. *Don't Retire, Rewire!* Indianapolis: Alpha Books, 2003.

Steingold, Fred S. *Legal Guidelines for Starting and Running a Small Business*. Berkeley, CA: Nolo Press, 2001.

Studies

Montenegro, Xenia; Fisher, Linda; and Remez, Shereen. *Staying Ahead of the Curve: The AARP Work and Career Study*. RoperASW, 2002.

I can't do it all plus fish!

From Morgan's story

*Clarify what you want to do, what really
turns you on. Focus, but let things evolve, too.
Revisit your choices continually.*

From Betsy's story

9

Rolling Up Your Sleeves
Serving the Community

*It is one of the most beautiful compensations of this life
that no man can sincerely try to help another
without helping himself.*
Ralph Waldo Emerson

Americans of all ages volunteer. We volunteer through
our churches, through federally sponsored organizations,
and through a vast variety of nonprofit associations.

Today, spokespersons for older Americans declare that
the experience of older adults shouldn't be lost or ignored,
but instead it should be used for positive societal change.
Marc Freedman, in *Prime Time: How Baby Boomers Will
Revolutionize Retirement and Transform America*, describes
how many older Americans are involved in service to the
community. These contributions are important in meeting
society's needs.

People who volunteer talk about the fulfillment they
gain through helping others. However, they cite many other
reasons for volunteering.

> ❗
> ◉ Volunteering through a nonprofit organization,
> a more formal commitment than helping out a friend
> or family member, offers some of the same benefits
> associated with paid work, plus the fulfillment of a
> desire to "give back."

Studies have shown that work is important to our mental and physical health to feel productive. Volunteering provides an opportunity to be productive—and to make a real difference.

Putting Beliefs and Skills into Action

During our lives we develop unique knowledge and skills. These are acquired through work, education, and personal experiences. Furthermore, we have concerns that are important to us. Volunteering provides an opportunity to be involved in what we do best or care about the most—while also giving back to our communities. Marilyn and Claudine demonstrate how we can put our beliefs and skills into action.

Giving Back—Marilyn's Story

Marilyn is a CPA and mother of five adult children. Helping women and children has always been her volunteer focus. While she was working she had limited time to volunteer. Since retiring at age 58, she uses her professional skills by serving on the boards of several organizations. One organization distributes money to help women become self-sufficient and another assists women who live in developing countries.

Because of her qualifications as a CPA, Marilyn often serves on boards as treasurer or as a member of the board's finance committee. But, she also assists low-income women with their tax returns. "I particularly enjoy seeing young people given opportunities and resources to learn," Marilyn says. "I look for organizations where I can use what I know from both my education and professional experience. I feel it's important to give back, [many] have not been as fortunate as I've been through life."

Skills and Interests Turned to Service— Claudine's Story

Claudine has worked as a business consultant and trainer. She volunteers based on what she enjoys doing and on her belief in the mission of an organization. One organization that meets these criteria is her local Food Bank. Claudine enjoys cooking and believes the Food Bank is administered well and meets the basic needs of the people it serves. As a member of the speakers' bureau for the Food Bank, she uses her skills as a presenter and talks to school groups. While acting as a chef's helper in cooking classes, she picks up tips from the chefs. She also introduces her grandchildren to volunteering by occasionally involving them in her work.

Claudine recently decided that she needs a stronger "feeling of purpose" and applied to the Peace Corps. She hopes to use her business skills to "make the world a little better," while enjoying the experience of international living.

Lessons from Marilyn and Claudine

Both Marilyn and Claudine have chosen to fulfill their life values through volunteer work. Marilyn works for groups that support women and children's issues. Claudine volunteers with organizations whose missions she supports. They both do what they enjoy and are skilled in, and they both feel productive.

> 👁 It's important to identify your reasons for volunteering. If you know what you want out of the experience, you're more likely to be satisfied. Do you want to continue using skills that you've honed over the years? If so, what are they? Do you have a cause that you're passionate about? If so, what is it?

Making New Friends or Business Contacts— Joe and Fern's Story

While in their mid-50s, Joe and his wife, Fern, whom you met in Chapter 5 about illness, decided to find a place to spend their retirement years. They wanted to work from five to ten years in that community, get to know it well, and then make a decision whether that's where they'd settle down to retire. They chose Aiken, South Carolina.

During his tenure as a superintendent of schools in South Carolina, Joe became active in such organizations as the Chamber of Commerce and the Presbyterian Church. He got to know key resource people in the community. After retirement from the school system, he consulted and taught part time until he learned he had cancer. Joe decided to retire, but he continues to do volunteer work.

The contacts he developed through community organizations during his first years in South Carolina continue to be important to him. Joe does Rotary work, and he gives volunteer assistance to the "Acts of Caring" Clinic (for those who are under insured) and the Salvation Army Boys and Girls Club. He's made a deliberate choice since retiring "to be far more involved in community life than I had planned." Joe feels that making a volunteer contribution enriches his life.

Fern retired when they moved to Aiken. After sorting out which organizations would meet her needs, she got involved in the volunteer community with hopes of making friends. Her choices included volunteer activities connected to her former work in hospitals such as the Red Cross. And because she enjoys the artistic work of other people, she also volunteers for local cultural arts organizations. The diversity of her volunteer work gives her a broad social network.

Joe and Fern knew they were in transition and purposely volunteered in order to make new friends and new business contacts.

Lessons from Joe and Fern

Meeting new people is helpful during times of transition. We may feel isolated when making changes as a result of a loss through death or divorce, a move to a new community, or a job change. Volunteering can help us reshape our lives by establishing a new network of friends or business contacts.

Fern first decided what her needs were, then selected organizations to match, and finally got involved and made friends. Following that sequence saved her a lot of time and effort because she didn't become involved with organizations in which she had no long-term interest. The exercise section of this chapter provides ways for you to narrow your choices of organizations.

Meeting new people can be interesting and beneficial at any time—not just during transitions. New contacts give fresh perspectives on life and often introduce us to new activities.

Exploring or Expanding an Area of Interest

Volunteering can also be an antidote to boredom and an opportunity to develop new skills. Some people volunteer for board and committee work in community-based organizations in order to make business contacts and become more skillful in group dynamics, meeting management, or public speaking. Others volunteer as a way to learn about organizations in their community or explore fields in which they are interested.

For example, we know of a former high-tech engineer who retired before he turned 50 and then developed a keen interest in bats. Now, as an active volunteer for the Audubon Society, he gives lectures to school children and leads field trips focused on bats.

Skill Building—Cindy's Story

Cindy, a self-employed carpenter and Jill-of-all-trades, learns new skills through volunteering. Until recently Cindy lived on a 39-foot sailboat. She and her husband, Jim, frequently spent three to six months in one location before moving on.

While in Annapolis one winter, she decided to volunteer at the local library. She offered to do anything they needed, and soon she was helping in the book repair area. By the time Cindy and Jim left Annapolis the following summer, she had learned the basics of bookbinding. A couple years later while their boat was tied up in a small town in Ireland, she volunteered at a bookbindery as a "casual apprentice" and further refined her skills. Now having sold their boat and bought a farm, she not only uses her bookbinding skills to produce unique gifts for her friends, but she's also starting to get commissioned jobs.

Lessons from Cindy

Cindy offers this advice to anyone thinking of volunteering as a way to learn a new skill: "Be bold and go after the experience you want to have. Treat volunteering like a real job."

The Benefits of Volunteering

The volunteers' stories in this chapter illustrate some of the benefits of volunteering. They demonstrate that you can focus on what you really want to do as well as experiment with new opportunities. Volunteering allows you to:

- Develop or improve your skills
- Meet new people
- Make contacts for business or other volunteer activities
- Gain experience in an area of interest
- Use your skills and education
- Put your beliefs into action
- Gain fulfillment through helping others

Getting Involved

The best-selling job-hunting book, *What Color is Your Parachute?* by Richard Bowles, identifies "What? Where? How?" as important questions to ask yourself when hunting for a job. These same questions apply to finding the right volunteer opportunity. You need to determine what skills you want to use, what you want to do as a volunteer, where you want to volunteer, and how you can find the right volunteer opportunity.

exercise►

What Skills Do You Want to Use?

During our lives most of us have prepared a resume—a summary of our experience, skills, and education. The first step toward volunteering is to prepare a summary of the skills (work *and* personal), education, and interests you want to use as a volunteer. (Refer to your Midlife Transitions Inventory in Part Four for ideas.) Use a blank sheet of paper for this exercise.

Example:
Skills, Interests, and Education Volunteer Resume

Work Skills:
Leading teams of people
Writing newsletters
Desktop publishing
Giving presentations

Personal Skills:
Speak Spanish fluently
Skiing
Cooking
Tutoring

Interests:
Other cultures
Art

Education:
Spanish major
Intercultural communication workshops
Masters in Business

exercise

What Do You Want to Do?

Now focus on what you want to do as a volunteer.
Answer the questions that are appropriate for you.

1. What skills do you want to use, develop or improve as a volunteer?

2. What kinds of new people do you want to meet as a volunteer?

3. What kinds of contacts for business or volunteer activities do you want to make?

4. What new area of interest do you want to gain experience in as a volunteer?

5. What knowledge do you want to use?

6. What beliefs do you want to put into action?

7. What kind of volunteer position do you want?

8. What level of responsibility do you want?

9. How much time do you want to contribute? What are your time restrictions? Day? Evening? Only certain months?

The Right Volunteer Opportunity

Based on your interests and the benefits you're seeking, the next step is to compile a list of the nonprofit organizations you want to investigate. There are resource directories of nonprofit organizations at your local library. Be sure to decide in what part of the city, state, country, or world you'd like to volunteer. If you want to assemble your own list, start by talking to your friends and contacts about what you want. They may give you some good leads. If you're interested in a specific organization, check to see if it has a website that will provide information, or just give them a call.

Many communities have a volunteer referral organization. There are also volunteer referral websites for organizations such as RSVP (Retired and Senior Volunteer Program for those 55+) or VolunteerMatch. Some local referral organizations give you the option of talking about your interests with a staff member or filling out an interest form online. Either way, they match what you want with the needs of local organizations and give you a list of options. Sometimes they also pave the way for you with the organization by letting them know you may be calling. Check for such local resources in the telephone directory under "Volunteer."

Your Savvy Sisters' Advice

- Determine which benefits of volunteering are important to you.
- Define the skills and interests you'd like to apply as a volunteer.
- Define the position you want and how much time you can commit.
- Research where you might want to volunteer.
- Now, just try it!

Resources to Help You Find the Right Volunteer Opportunity

Books

Blaustein, Arthur. *Make a Difference: America's Guide to Volunteering and Community Service.* San Francisco: Jossey Bass, 2003.

Bowles, Richard Nelson. *What Color is Your Parachute?* 2007. Berkeley: Ten Speed Press, 2006. (Revised and updated yearly.)

Canfield, Jack; Hansen, Mark Victor; McGraw Oberst, Arline; Boal, John and Lagana, Laura. *Chicken Soup for the Volunteer's Soul: Stories to Celebrate the Spirit of Courage, Caring and Community.* Deerfield Beach, FL: Health Communication, 2002.

Collins, Joseph; DeZerega, Stefano and Heckscher, Zahara. *How to Live Your Dream of Volunteering Overseas.* New York: Penguin Books, 2002.

Freedman, Marc. *Prime Time: How Baby Boomers Will Revolutionize Retirement and Transform America.* New York: Public Affairs, 1999.

Pidgeon, Walter P., Jr. *The Universal Benefits of Volunteering.* New York: John Wiley, 1998.

Websites

- www.airlineamb.org
  Airline Ambassadors provide help to children in other countries.

- www.elderhostel.org
  Elderhostel volunteers are involved in both domestic and international projects.

- www.escus.org
  Executive Service Corps, a nonprofit and public service agency.

- www.experiencecorps.org
  Experience Corps, with an orientation on children and youth.
- www.habitat.org
  Habitat for Humanity, with a focus on housing and homelessness.
- www.peacecorps.org
  Peace Corps, international programs.
- www.score.org
  SCORE (Service Corps of Retired Executives) Association focuses on helping small businesses succeed.
- www.seniorcorps.org
  Retired and Senior Volunteer Program (RSVP) for volunteers over 55 years of age.
- www.serviceleader.org
  Volunteer online.
- www.volunteerabroad.com
  Directory of volunteer abroad programs worldwide.
- www.VolunteerMatch.org
  VolunteerMatch, a national referral service.

10

Burned Out and Rekindled
Creativity and Learning

There is a quickening, a vitality, a life force that is translated through you into action, and because there is only one of you in all of time, this expression is unique.
Martha Graham

Although the above quote from the dancer Martha Graham doesn't use the word *creativity*, it captures its essence. To be creative is to be original, unique, to do something in a way that has never been done before. Those who are attentive to the stirrings of their spirit and become adept at hearing their own inner voice, tap the life force Graham describes and the world calls creativity.

Gene Cohen, author of *The Creative Age: Awakening Human Potential in the Second Half of Life*, defines creativity as "our innate capacity for growth," and he says everyone has this potential. Some of us are "big C" creative people who express our creativity formally through the arts and sciences. We have an audience for our work and may make our living being creative.

There are many of us who are "little c" creative. We express creativity on the job, in the kitchen, the garden, the workshop, through crafts and the way we decorate our homes, by composing a song, writing a poem, or by inventing a better mousetrap. The list is endless.

Creativity Knows No Age

Sarah Bernhardt, Sigmund Freud, Frank Lloyd Wright, Mahatma Gandhi, Toni Morrison, Virginia Wolf, Eleanor Roosevelt, and Nelson Mandela, to name a few, produced creative works after 50. But, by 50 some of us have run out of dreams and feel anything but creative.

Fortunately, creativity is a process that can be started at any time. It's a way of thinking and of doing. It can become an important part of developing expanded meaning in our lives. *Anything you do, can be done creatively.* Unfortunately, because many of us don't think of ourselves as even "little c" creatives, we must first hush the internal, judging voices that tell us we're wasting our time, we'll never be creative. Then, we must learn to let go and create space in our lives to let creativity in.

Finding Your Creative Voice—Margie's Story

For some people, being creative is a natural way of life; for others it has meant taking risks and making deliberate life choices. Margie was 26 when she became a fire and casualty agent. For 20 years she worked hard and eventually owned her own agency. She was a star, but she was also disillusioned, tired, and developing health problems. With "no clue" to what she would do, she took a buy out from her company.

Like others we described in Chapter 6 about transitions, Margie embarked on a transition, in her case for two and a half years. Leaving her job was "agonizing." Her identity was wrapped up in being a successful insurance agent with a position in the community, respect, income, and influence. "If I'm not that person, who am I?" she asked herself.

She describes this process as "having the shields and armor torn off" her psyche, but it allowed her to connect with others and herself in a way she had not previously done. The agonizing opened her up; it was a time of spiritual growth. She was afraid but realized she had a choice: She could live life in fear or in faith, and she had faith that the next step would appear.

The next step did appear in the form of an art therapist who helped her realize she was a creative person—an artist. Margie started writing poetry and evolved into a writer. "My throat filled up with words, and poems came out fully formed," she says.

For Margie "art is the creative expression of the spirit," and it has become her life's work. For inspiration she credits Martha Graham's quote at the beginning of the chapter and a female mentor who told her, "Each day, each moment, make a commitment to your dream." She writes those words on every page of her appointment book, and at 50, she has become a creativity coach. Her goal in the workshops she conducts, on creativity, creative writing, collage, and journaling, is to create an environment where people feel safe to be creative.

Lessons from Margie

Before Margie found her own form of creative expression, she had to face the fears that were holding her back. Over time her creativity evolved.

> ❗
> ◉ To hear your creative, inner voice you must learn to be still and tap your unconscious.

We offer some techniques in Resources to help you learn this skill.

Why is Creativity Important at Midlife?

Creativity not only contributes to our pleasure, it also contributes to our physical health. Creativity fosters positive feelings and well-being, which in turn promotes positive immune function, says Gene Cohen.

Aaron's story illustrates how the encouraging of our own and others' creativity can lead to a healthier life.

Creativity and Well-being—Aaron's Story

At 49 Aaron has a thriving business as a children's book illustrator, painter, and art teacher. He will paint 150 pictures this year and be featured in two gallery shows. Aaron and his wife live simply so they can sustain a creative lifestyle into the future. "I can't imagine not doing this forever" he says. "As long as I have the physical ability, I will continue painting. There is no pot of gold at the end of the rainbow that is more attractive than what I have today."

What Aaron has today was hard won. He always loved art, but rejection of a painting he submitted to an arts festival judge caused his confidence to falter. At 18, convinced he had no talent, he turned away from painting and became a printer. It was a transient life; he had 30 different jobs while in the trade. He was also abusing alcohol and drugs and finally bottomed-out in San Francisco. "Not much about my living skills was working for me," he says. He turned to Alcoholics Anonymous (AA) and believes it saved his life. "I learned what power I had over my life and tried to figure out what I wanted my life to be."

Aaron wanted to be self-employed. Plus, he'd gone a long time without painting and knew he wanted to start "doing art" again. In AA, Aaron had learned to "listen to my inner voice." That voice led him to move to a new city and take classes at a museum art school. For four years he worked full time as a printer and painted the rest of the time. An instructor, "who saw something in me, I didn't see in myself," inspired him and convinced him he had the persistence necessary to be an artist. "I was finally becoming a real person—myself—and I finally had something to say."

At first Aaron had trouble calling himself an artist, but when he sold his first painting, he believed it. "That got even with the professor who told me I had no talent when I was 18," he says. When he was able to let go of the mindset that his income could only come from printing, opportunities came to him. He quit the printing business and became a full-time artist and teacher.

Aaron tells his students that he's an example of a successful artist, but not an exception. He tells them they also have all the tools necessary to create art.

Lessons from Aaron

Aaron and Margie didn't initially consider themselves creative. Creativity emerged for them out of their life struggles. But the lesson they both learned was that they had always been creative—it was a matter of *believing* they could be. Aaron believes "people have many creative options with their lives, but it's up to the individual to go after them."

> **!**
> ◉ When we're young or just starting to flex our creative muscles, we're particularly vulnerable to criticism. We must learn to put criticism in perspective by having faith in ourselves, choosing to ignore the criticism, or by getting a variety of opinions. Also, we must learn skills to hush our "inner critic," who may be the most severe critic of all.

Continuous Learning

Learning helps some of us discover our creativity. We often need education, as well as self-knowledge, for our personal development. For some, continuous learning is essential to staying current and professionally competent. Others take courses to explore new interests or to focus more deeply on specific subjects.

Some older students return to college after years in the workforce in order to make a career change or to finish a degree program they started earlier. Part-time higher education enrollments more than doubled between 1970 and 2000. A majority of those students are undergraduate students age 35 and over completing traditional or online degrees. Ursula's story is a case in point.

Going Back to College—Ursula's Story

When she was 50, Ursula invited her elderly mother to live with her. Over the next several years, she watched her mother "die year by year by giving up things. She gave up gardening. She didn't want to get up in the morning; she didn't care anymore." Ursula became aware that she didn't want to turn into her mom and "give up." What Ursula was most concerned about giving up was learning.

Years passed and then two years ago, in her 70s, Ursula made a big decision—she wanted to get a college degree. She wanted and needed to be paid for the kind of work she did as a volunteer. She was bored and wanted to use her brain more and her TV less. Perhaps the most important reason Ursula wanted to go back to school was that she wanted to be a model for her children. She thought about her mother and how she had given up on life. She wanted her children to know, "It's never too late to get your education."

Ursula is majoring in human services. She was successful in getting financial aid for her tuition, and she's learning to navigate the academic system—parking, enrollment, and class selection. While she knew how to use a computer, she had to learn new software and how to use the Internet for research. Ursula's advice to others who are going back to school is, "Never stop learning and don't give up."

Lessons from Ursula

Ursula needed to parlay her volunteer experience into paid work and felt she needed a degree to do this credibly. She realized that staying mentally active was important for a healthy old age and wanted to be a good example to her children. She has worked hard to overcome the stumbling blocks she encountered when she returned to college.

Education to Change Careers—Daniel's Story

Ursula wanted a college degree. But, some people need a shorter program, often a certificate program from a university or a focused community college degree, in order to advance their careers or prepare for a job change.

Daniel, whom you met in Chapter 6 about transitions, was bored with his job as a U. S. Public Health Service administrator and hoped to take early retirement. At that time, he'd developed an interest in bodywork such as yoga, Rolfing, Tai Chi, and massage. As his knowledge increased, it occurred to him that some form of bodywork might be the basis of a second career, after he retired. He investigated programs in his area and settled on a three-year occupational therapy program at a local community college. Working full time and going to school wasn't easy, but when retirement was available to him, he was able to take it and slide right into a second career.

Lessons from Daniel

Daniel did two important things: He looked to his interests and hobbies as the basis for a job change. And, although he already had a Masters degree, he developed a plan for getting the additional education he needed to be qualified for his new career.

> **!**
> ◉ People who both work and go to school must make sacrifices in time, energy, and money. Some employers provide tuition reimbursement for classes that benefit employees in their present job, but few, if any, employers will pay to train you for a new career. So, if your midlife education must be self-funded, consider it an important investment in your future.

Learning for Fun

Not all adult learners are after grades or degrees. Many take advantage of courses at four-year and community colleges to pursue new interests or delve more deeply into a subject they didn't have time for earlier in life such as learning Spanish or becoming an expert in renaissance music.

Others enroll in "learning-in-retirement-institutes" offered on college campuses by organizations such as Elderhostel. The motivation for these learners is intellectual stimulation, gaining interest related skills, or social contact with people who have similar interests.

Elderhostel offers programs to individuals 55 and over. (If your spouse is 55, but you're younger, you qualify to attend too.) Many of these programs provide opportunities for combined learning and travel at reasonable prices.

Your Savvy Sisters' Advice

- Use your creativity. It increases your self-esteem and helps you reinvent yourself at midlife. It can be an antidote to the fear of losing your identity if and when you leave your career.

- Experiment with new interests through classes and self-study. You may gain a hobby or discover a new career.

- Investigate online programs if you'd like to get a degree from home.

- Learn new things. It literally stimulates your brain and may be a deterrent to dementia and Alzheimer's.

Encourage your Creativity

No matter how you want to apply your creativity—gardening, painting, writing, woodworking, crafts, etc.—here is an exercise to raise your creative consciousness that Julia Cameron, author of *The Artist's Way*, recommends to get you started.

- Set aside one or two hours a week to do something alone that "nurtures your creative consciousness, your inner artist."

- Use the time to visit a gallery or museum, take a walk, go to the beach, or wander through a bookstore. Whatever you do, the point is that you do it *alone* and that you hold the time sacred.

Listen to your Inner Voice

Margie and Aaron, as well as others we interviewed for this book, described how they gained insight about what was important to them by listening to their inner voice. Both Natalie Goldberg, author of *Writing Down the Bones*, and Julia Cameron recommend daily writing to silence the inner judge who tells you you're not creative. Here's an exercise to help you learn how to listen to your inner, creative voice.

- For ten minutes, or three pages, start writing—anything that comes to mind.

- Don't stop and think—just keep writing.

- Don't worry if it's nice, polite, or politically correct—just keep writing.

- Be specific. Don't say "tree," say "maple." Don't say "feelings," say "sad" or "angry."

- Don't worry about spelling, punctuation, or grammar—just keep writing.

- "Go for the jugular," Goldberg says. "If something comes up that is scary or naked, dive right into it."

- Don't let anyone else see your writing. It's just for you.

exercise▶

Courses in your Future Quiz

Think about the results of your Midlife Values Inventory in Chapter 6 and your Midlife Transitions Inventory in Part Four, and then answer these questions:

- Do you have interests or hobbies that might be the basis for a job change? If so, what might this new job be?

- What, if any, education would you need to prepare yourself for this job change?

- Do you have interests or hobbies you'd like to explore more fully? Are there classes or programs that could help you do this? If so, what and where are they?

- As you think about the values that are important to you now, or that may be important to you in the future, do you anticipate that you'll want to continue your education? If so, how?

Resources to Explore and Expand Your Creativity and Learning

Books

Bear, John B. and Bear, Mariah P. *Bear's Guide to Earning Degrees by Distance Learning*. Berkeley: Ten Speed Press, 2001.

Bear, John B. and Bear, Mariah P. *College Degrees by Mail and Internet*. Berkeley: Ten Speed Press, 2001.

Cameron, Julia. *The Artist's Way*. New York: J. P. Tarcher, 2002.

Cohen, Gene. *The Creative Age: Awakening Human Potential in the Second Half of Life*. New York: Avon Books, 2000.

Goleman, Daniel; Kaufman, Paul; and Ray, Michael. *The Creative Spirit*. New York: Penguin Books, 1992.

Edwards, Betty. *The New Drawing on the Right Side of the Brain*. New York: J. P. Tarcher, 1999.

Goldberg, Natalie. *Writing Down the Bones: Freeing the Writer Within*. Boston: Shambala Press, 1986.

Gregory, Danny. *The Creative License*. New York: Hyperion, 2006.

Hudson, Frederic M. *The Adult Years: Mastering the Art of Self-Renewal*. San Francisco: Jossey-Bass, 1999.

Lamdin, Lois. *Earn College Credit for What You Know*. Dubuque: Kendall/Hunt Publishing Company, 1997. A good resource if you are thinking of going to college to earn a degree.

Lamott, Ann. *Bird by Bird: Some Instructions for Writing and Life*. New York: Doubleday, 1994.

Tharp, Twyla. *The Creative Habit: Learn It and Use It for Life*. New York: Simon and Schuster, 2005.

Yamaguchi, Jeffrey. 52 Projects: Random Acts of Creativity. New York: Berkley Publishing Group, 2005.

Websites

- www.elderhostel.com
  Elderhostel—Adventures in Life Long Learning

11

On the Road
Traveling

*We will travel as far as we can, but we cannot
in one lifetime see all that we would see,
or learn all that we hunger to know.*
Loren Eiseley

Many of us have a passion for travel. We seek adventure, romance, and relaxation through travel. We travel to learn and provide service. We attend festivals, family reunions, and sports events.

Some of us travel extensively on business, but weekends and vacations are often used for fun travel. For some of us, once we have more time or are able to make more time, travel becomes the central theme of our lives. Travel can be an extension of our interests or can even lead to a new lifestyle.

Fran, Charline, and Joan all love to travel, but their stories illustrate different approaches to blending travel with work at midlife.

Time Limitations—Fran's Story

Fran and Bob, her husband, both 51 and working full time, have always enjoyed travel. Early in their married lives they camped and "traveled on the cheap," usually in the United States. Now they have more money for travel, but they're limited by Bob's work schedule. His vacation time falls during the height of the summer tourist season, when fares are expensive.

They like to visit foreign countries and have learned from experience that they prefer small towns to big cities. Their preference is to stay in one place and take their time exploring from that base. Often they're bird-watching or practicing their golf swings.

They used to stay in bed and breakfasts (B & B's) or small country hotels. But a few years ago they discovered the perfect travel solution to their time and money limitations: house swapping. Working through an agency (see Resources), they swap houses with families in Europe or North America. A house exchange satisfies their need for a base and lets them get a feel for life in another country or place. Their trip is enriched through meeting the neighbors, friends, and family of the people whose homes they have exchanged for theirs.

Lessons from Fran

Fran and Bob thought about what they like best about traveling: their preferred lodging, activities, and pace. Then they found creative options for satisfying their travel dreams, even with limited time and money.

Less Work, More Travel—Charline's Story

Charline loves her work as a program officer for a major charitable foundation, but international travel has become her passion. Recently she negotiated with her manager and was able to modify her position to three-quarters time (nine months a year). She now takes three one-month trips each year, but works very long hours in order to maintain her credibility as a senior administrator.

What attracts Charline to travel? "When I start to think about a new trip, my heart beats faster and my everyday world seems like such a pleasant place. I can make one trip last two years. I love the planning, the research, and buying books. You talk to people and then you go—and you can talk about it forever."

For 24 years, Charline and her husband, Ernie, spent their weekends and vacations in the woods, hiking and backpacking. Then Charline felt "time clicking away" and decided it was time for them to travel together internationally. They started with a strenuous bicycling trip through the Outer Hebrides of Scotland the next year. Kayaking in Baja California to ward off the winter blahs followed that. Recently they took a group-hiking trip through the Pyrenees Mountains.

Lessons from Charline

Long hours are sometimes required to maintain a career combined with travel. Charline and Ernie have wisely chosen to do their physically taxing adventure travel while they're still both healthy and physically able. Charline realizes that travel, and planning for travel, gives her optimism that she carries over to the rest of her life.

A New Lifestyle—Your Savvy Sister Joan's Story

Some people such as your Savvy Sister Joan, and her husband, Neil, are so enthralled with travel that it has become the major theme of their lives. This is Joan's story.

I like learning about other cultures and languages, eating strange food, and getting into unpredictable situations. Neil and I spend our discretionary funds on travel, not on the latest cars or a second home. Early in our marriage his work took us to Latin America and

Europe. These experiences whetted our appetites for international living and travel.

In our late 40s we decided to forego career advancement in order to have the flexibility of more time for travel. We traveled widely in Europe, Latin America, and Southeast Asia, usually with our suitcase packs on our backs. We studied Spanish, taught English in Mexico, and represented an international partnership program in Costa Rica. We travel because we love art and history, and we want to learn about other cultures. Like Charline, the challenge and enjoyment of travel give us the energy we need for the rest of the year.

Two years ago we again rebalanced our work and travel lives. We bought a 20-year old boat in Holland and now live on it every summer, cruising the inland waterways of Europe. This is a surprisingly inexpensive way to live, as long as we don't eat out a lot. We now dedicate the summer months to travel and the rest of the year to part-time work.

Lessons from Joan

After assessing their work/life balance, Joan and Neil elected to pay a price professionally and financially so that they could do more of what they loved—travel. However, they caution that it's important to carefully assess the consequences before making what could be an irreversible career move.

!

◉ Those who yearn for extensive travel should weigh the pros and cons. The pros are easy to enumerate: adventure, learning, and enjoyment. The cons are sometimes more difficult to recognize or acknowledge: missing family and friends, putting your work and home life on hold, and the general discomforts of travel. But, the bottom line for most inveterate travelers is: *They wouldn't want it any other way.*

Options for Travel

Charline and Joan plan their own trips, make all the arrangements, and travel extensively on an independent basis. They have also studied and done service work abroad. Most people, like Fran and Bob, focus on shorter trips. Many prefer having someone help them with the planning process or being part of a group while traveling.

The travel industry has created a wide range of options for people of all ages, energy levels, and interests. No longer are packaged vacations structured and unimaginative. Many innovative travel providers offer customized trips at a good price. Check with your travel agent or use the Internet to find the best package for you.

Nonprofit organizations such as alumni associations, the Smithsonian Institution, and local clubs or community colleges also offer appealing options. Elderhostel, for people 55 and over, operates more than 1,000 one-week stays at learning institutions around the world. Participants usually stay on or near a campus. Each stay focuses on a theme, with classes taught by experts.

There are also organizations that offer structured volunteer service experiences. Some of the more interesting options we've discovered are in Resources. Domestic and international travel is available at all prices and levels of simplicity or luxury.

The thought of travel, especially to international locations, can be intimidating even for people who travel often. Books on travel are available at your local library and the travel sections of bookstores. Travel books are usually focused on a particular location or a type of travel such as adventure, cruises, and walking trips. Many provide information on the history, art, and culture of the area, as well as weather charts and other practical tips. These can be useful for your itinerary planning.

Short courses on travel offered by community colleges, and conversations with your traveling friends, can increase your knowledge and your psychological comfort level for any type of travel. Don't forget the incredible resources now available on the Internet. Just key your area of interest into a search engine such as Google, and you'll find many options to explore.

Travel Planning

Have you ever returned from a trip and discovered you missed a special museum? Or did you find out too late that you were only a few miles from "the best small beach in the country"? Planning will help you avoid disappointment.

Planning doesn't mean being "rigid" or "inflexible." In fact, the more organized your trip, the more relaxed you'll be and the more fun you can have. The way to have carefree travel is to prepare for it in advance. Planning will help you minimize the problems that might occur, and you'll be better able to handle those that do.

 Your Savvy Sisters' Advice

- Experiment with different types of travel until you find the right fit for you. For example, don't let anyone talk you into a safari if you're a city person.

- Get started as soon as you can because your options for travel may decrease as you grow older.

- Plan. You'll get more out of your experience.

Getting the Most Out of Travel

We recommend six important steps to help you get the most out of travel:

1. Daydream about where you'd like to go.

2. Think about specific things you'd like to do.

3. Decide if you want to travel alone or with someone.

4. Determine if you have sufficient time and money.

5. Plan an itinerary.

6. Then, make reservations and arrangements.

The next several sections provide suggestions or exercises for each of these steps.

Travel Daydreaming

Even for a business trip or a long weekend holiday, think about, and, yes, fantasize about, where you'd like to go, places you'd like to visit, and things you'd like to do. Your dreaming phase can also help you focus on special events (New Orleans Jazz Festival), or parts of the world (Italy), or themes (cooking) that call to you.

exercise

Travel Daydreaming Quiz

Reviewing your results of the Midlife Values Inventory in Chapter 6 and the Midlife Transitions Inventory in Part Four may give you some new ideas about travel themes or destinations. Now, sit back, relax, and answer the following questions:

Where do you dream of going?

What is your trip theme or objective?

What would make your trip a success?

Places to Visit/Things to Do

Now expand your ideas of where you'd like to go. If you want to go to Paris, do you want to visit museums, sidewalk cafes, or churches? What activities or places would relate to your trip theme or objective?

Take out a blank sheet of paper and jot down your ideas for special places you'd like to visit and things you'd like to do.

Travel Partners

Some people enjoy traveling with others; some prefer traveling alone. The wrong travel partner can ruin a trip.

> ◉ Different destinations or travel objectives may call for different traveling companions. If you want to travel with someone, identify your ideal companion for the trip you have in mind, *before approaching a specific person*. Consider energy level, attitude, personality, and flexibility.

If you decide to travel with someone—including your spouse or partner—identify what's important to each of you. Talk about the kinds of activities that appeal to each of you: visiting art museums, taking pictures, visiting relatives, going to concerts, hiking, etc. Make sure your travel partner completes the preceding exercises, and then compare and discuss the results.

Time and Money

You may have the option of planning your "trip of a lifetime" without constraints, but more frequently time and money put limits on your dreams. It's important to estimate the major costs of your proposed trip. Usually your major trip expenses will be for transportation, lodging, food, and special arrangements. If you're traveling with someone, make adjustments so that you agree on a general mode of travel (luxury, moderate, or economy) and are both comfortable with the budget.

Determine how much time you have for a trip. If you have a travel partner, make sure you are in agreement not only on the number of days, but also on the week or month you plan to travel. Sometimes the most complex part of trip planning is coordinating schedules.

exercise▶

Travel Reality Quiz

Before moving on to the next steps, and while the planning process is still flexible, it's a good idea to do a reality check.

- Do you want to travel independently, with a partner, or with a group?

- Do you know what would make this trip a success for you—and for your traveling partner?

- Have you decided on a schedule?

- Have you decided on a mode of travel—luxury, moderate, or economy?

- Is the cost of the trip within your budget?

- Have you discussed all these issues with your traveling partner, if you have one?

Next Steps

Building a travel itinerary and making reservations are the next steps. Trip planning organizations or travel agents will help you with these steps, but at a price. The big advantage is that someone else worries about all the details. For some people such as Charline, travel research and planning are a source of great enjoyment, and they want to do it themselves.

If you have little travel experience and want to learn how to do your own research and planning, you might plan part of your trip yourself and have a travel agent or organization do the rest. For example, if you decide to go on an organized tour that provides an option of independent travel days after the scheduled events, you could research and plan the optional days yourself.

Most importantly, do what you enjoy!

Resources to Help You Get Started and Get the Most Enjoyment from Travel

Books

Benson, Sam. *Don't Let the World Pass You By! 52 Reasons to Have a Passport*. Footscray, Australia: Lonely Planet Publications, 2005.

Consumer Reports. *Consumer Reports Travel Well for Less: Smart Travel Planning in the US and Abroad*, 2002.

Heilman, Joan Rattner. *Unbelieveably Good Deals and Great Adventures That You Absolutely Can't Get Unless You're Over 50, 2007-2008 ed.* NY: McGraw Hill, 2007.

Krannich, Ronald, and Krannich, Caryl Rae. *Jobs for People Who Love to Travel: Opportunities at Home and Abroad*. Manassas Park, VA: Impact Publications, 1999.

Krannich, Ronald and Krannich, Caryl Rae. *Travel Planning on the Internet: The Click and Easy Guide*. Manassas Park, VA: Impact Publications, 2000.

Let's Go Roadtripping USA: The Complete Coast-to-Coast Guide to America. Cambridge, MA: Let's Go Publications, 2005.

McMillon, Bill; Crutchins, Doug and Geissenger, Anne. *Volunteer Vacations, 9th ed.* Chicago: Chicago Review Press, 2006

Schultz, Patricia. *1,000 Places to See Before You Die.* New York: Workman Publishing, 2003.

Steves, Rick. *Rick Steves Europe Through the Back Door 2007: The Travel Skills Handbook.* Emeryville, CA: Avalon Travel Publishing, 2006.

Websites

- www.elderhostel.org
  Elderhostel: An organization offering residential learning programs for those over 55.

- www.globalvolunteers.org
  Global Volunteers: An organization that sends volunteers to several countries for one to two weeks.

- www.habitat.org
  Habitat for Humanity: Volunteers involved in hands-on home building work around the world.

- www.idealist.org/travel
  Links to organizations that specialize in placing volunteers in different countries.

- www.intervac.com
  Intervac: An international home-exchange holiday service.

- www.peacecorps.gov
  Peace Corps: Volunteers spend two years in one of 80 countries.

- www.WiredSeniors.com
  Services to help people over 50 find a traveling companion.

Our Favorite Series of Travel Guides

- Lonely Planet Guides
- Michelin Green Guides
- Rick Steves' Guides

When I start to think about a new trip,
my heart beats faster and my everyday world
seems like such a pleasant place.

From Charline's story

Part Five

People Needing People

Good relationships are the most powerful contributor to our happiness, according to a recent study by psychologists Ed Diener and Martin Seligman. They found that those who have close friends and strong family relationships are happier than those who don't.

When we think about making changes in our lives such as accepting a new job, starting to work from home, traveling more, developing new interests, or retiring, we need to consider how these changes may affect our relationships. The interests we previously shared with a partner or friends may change, or our schedules may differ. We may no longer share the same values. So, how do we maintain these friendships? How do we adjust our marriage relationship? How do we make friends to share new interests?

A special concern for those of us at midlife is how to juggle the responsibilities of our work, family, and personal lives in order to care for our aging parents. It is no longer common for our parents to live with us in their old age. However, as we take on any care-giving relationship with our parents, we must plan for the emotional, physical, and financial implications.

Hopefully, by midlife we have all learned that good relationships require time and tending—they don't happen automatically. Therefore, we think it's important that you include them in Your Life After 50 Plan.

12

Social Ties
Friends and Family

*Nobody sees a flower—really — it is so small
it takes time—we haven't time and to see takes time,
like to have a friend takes time.*
Georgia O'Keeffe

People who have friends are happier than those who don't. Life without friends is no fun. With all the benefits of friendship, it's worth considering who our friends are and how we can improve the quality of our friendships as we plan for life after 50.

We make friends throughout our lives. Some of our friendships began in grade school, in high school, or in college. Some friendships endure forever, and some are situational.

Usually our friendships are based on sharing a common interest such as the arts, the outdoors, sports, or politics. We make friends through work, church, community, and other friends. Our friends may be the parents of our kids' friends or the people with whom we exercise. Some of us have few, if any, family ties within our communities, and friends may replace family for traditions such as Thanksgiving or Christmas dinner. Friends often satisfy a need for psychological support. But keeping friendships alive is not easy.

While our parents' friendships were often based on a lifetime of shared experiences with family or friends in their communities, we have, as baby boomers, moved more frequently than our parents did. With every move we gained and lost friends. And as important as friendships are to our well-being, our hectic lives can prevent spending much time nurturing and developing those friendships. This is especially true if we are working full time and busy with our spouse and children. Also, the attention that friendships receive may differ based on gender.

Women's Friendships

Women are more apt than men to nurture friendships. Women tend to have friends who meet the needs of the various stages of their lives. At midlife, many of us are in transition, and our friends help us see facets of ourselves we can't even imagine. It may be difficult for our families to see us in new roles or with new interests, and they may find it even more difficult to encourage us to change. Our friends provide the encouragement and emotional support we need to move forward with our lives.

A recent study, described in *The Psychological Review*, suggests that a woman's friends may be important to her happiness by helping her counteract stress. The researchers found that women physiologically respond differently than men do to stress. When a woman is under stress, the oxytocin hormone is released. This hormone counters the fight or flight response we associate with stress and encourages her to draw closer to friends and children. When she is interacting with children and friends, more of the hormone is released. This interaction "further counters stress and produces a calming effect."

Women's Friendships—Evelyn and Betty's Stories

There are many ways women develop and maintain friendships. Evelyn and Betty's stories describe some of these.

Evelyn works for the Chamber of Commerce in Washington, D.C. and has a busy professional life. As a single woman, she fears being isolated as she grows older. It's important to her to have a close circle of women friends, so she does the work to maintain those ties. She makes the plans for outings with others such as getting tickets to the theatre or arranging group dinners. She also realizes that no group of friends is static, and she works at adding new friends to her circle.

Betty found that after her husband died, many of her friends in San Diego no longer contacted her. As a single person, she was no longer included in the couples' gatherings that were a significant part of her and her husband's social life.

But, earlier in life, Betty had learned, "You can't sit back and wait for people to come to you. You have to get out and do something, even if it hurts." She decided to move to the town where her son lived, start a new life, and make new friends. There, she got involved as a volunteer in several organizations: PFLAG (Parents, Family, and Friends of Gays and Lesbians), the Unitarian Fellowship, and the local theatre. Her hard work was rewarded. Now, seven years later, she has remarried and is quite satisfied with her life and her friendships.

Lessons from Evelyn and Betty

Friendships require work; they need to be nurtured. Sometimes circumstances change the basis of a friendship. For example, friendships may wither when one person moves to a new location, loses interest in a shared activity, or loses a spouse through divorce or death.

> ❗
> 👁 There is something serendipitous about developing
> new friendships. There must be "chemistry" between two
> people as well as common interests. However, we can
> put ourselves in situations where developing new friends
> is more likely.

Men's Friendships—Mort and Fred's Stories

Studies show that, compared to women, men are likely
to have fewer close, enduring friendships. Men often
develop informal friendships through sports, membership
in clubs, or hobbies. Some men have strong ties with their
co-workers, but the basis of such friendships revolves
around work interests. When a job ends, so may the
friendships. The most enduring friendships men develop
are often during times of shared intensity such as their
college years or military service. As men grow older,
however, shared interests may draw them together.

Mort, a physician who retired at 56 from his medical
practice, moved to a new community and became active
in the Masonic Lodge. He stays tied to his former
profession through a journal review club with other
arthritis specialists. In addition, he belongs to a men's
group that meets monthly to discuss a focused topic such
as a book or a problem one of the members is having.
He acknowledges that the men's group serves as "a little
bit of a support group."

The Harvard Study of Adult Development that George
Valliant discusses in *Aging Well* shows that when men are
isolated socially, that isolation may lead to death at an
earlier age. Yet, as they grow older, beyond the competition
of youth and early adulthood, some men learn to support
each other and keep each other's dreams alive.

Fred, who has a seminar and coaching business, has maintained close friendships over the last 22 years. He relied on several close friends and his men's group for support through his employment changes and a difficult divorce. Fred found that while his close friends provided the most support, "the men's group is good for talking things out. It has been part of my learning about change." The group gets together regularly to discuss issues that are important in their lives—parenting, relationships, work, and aging. Fred uses friends for emotional support and perspective on life's issues.

Lessons from Mort and Fred

Professional ties can lead to closer friendships at midlife. Some men find that having a group of friends who have a broad set of interests is rewarding intellectually and psychologically.

> ❗ ◈ If developing and nurturing friendships wasn't a priority for you during the career-building phase of your life, there is substantial evidence that it's worth the effort at midlife.

Family

Some of us find our most satisfying friendships with family members. We enjoy their companionship, provide mutual emotional support, or simply share memories. Siblings and children can be our strongest support as we grow older. For some of us, our spouse or partner is our best friend. These friendships become more significant as we deal with the problems of our own aging or that of family members.

Grandchildren also play a significant role in many of our lives and may even determine where we live.

We may or may not want to baby-sit grandchildren, but most grandparents want to spend time with them and get to know them without the same responsibilities they felt as parents.

Building and Maintaining Friendships

You may be thinking, "But I don't have many friends." Perhaps you've never thought about how friendships are formed or maintained or the importance of friendship for your health and happiness. Remember, too, that all of our friends need not have the same characteristics. We may enjoy playing tennis with one friend but share an interest in reading with another. Occasionally we are lucky enough to have a friend who is a soul mate.

Reach out to those with interests similar to yours to develop new friendships. Sharing your interests with others will also enhance your enjoyment and involvement in new activities. Remember, each person needs to put effort into a friendship and initiate contact on a regular basis.

Betty and Mort learned the benefits of joining groups when they each moved to a new community. They took the initiative to become active in organizations and subsequently made friends. Whether or not you're new to your community, if you want to develop new friends, take classes, join clubs, or volunteer.

As our lives change we also need to work on maintaining existing friendships. It's important to make time for old friends through regularly scheduled meetings, whether for a long walk or a cup of coffee. Friendship is a powerful contributor to our health and happiness.

Your Savvy Sisters' Advice

- Appreciate what your friends mean to you. Find ways to let them know they're valued.

- Work at the friendships you want to maintain. Make frequent contact, share activities, and spend special occasions together.

- Focus on the needs of your friends. Notice what's important to them and try to please them.

- Work on your listening skills. Address any problems in your relationships.

- Make new friends with both men and women *of all ages.*

- Don't idealize friendship and expect it to be without disappointments.

exercise▶

Friendship Survey

The following survey will help you think about your friendships, their current status, and how they might change in your life after 50. The survey may also prompt some ideas about how to go about making new friends or reinforcing your current friendships.

exercise

Friendship Survey

1. Make a list on a blank sheet of paper: Who are the people you are closest to and regard as friends?

2. Answer these questions for each person on the list:

   a. What is the basis for your friendship?

   b. Is this a work friend? If you change your job, will this friendship last? How will you make it last?

   c. If you move, will this friendship endure? How will you make it endure?

   d. What do you currently do to maintain and nurture this friendship?

   e. What more could you do?

3. Who else would you like on your list of friends? What types of interests would he or she have? Where might you meet this person?

4. Review your list of friends and the comments you made. Think about the importance of friendship to your health and happiness.

Resources to Help You Better Understand How to Make and Keep Friends

Articles

Blieszner, Rosemary. "'She'll Be on My Heart': Intimacy Among Friends." *Generations* (Summer 2001): 48-54.

Diener, Ed and Seligman, Martin. "Very Happy People." *Psychological Science* (2002) 13: 81-84.

Dorfman, Lorraine. "Retirement and Family Relationships: An Opportunity in Later Life." *Generations* (Summer 2002): 74-79.

Taylor, S.E., Klein, L.C., Lewis, B.P., Gruenewald, T.L., Gurung, R.A.R., and Undegraff, J.A. "Female Responses to Stress: Tend and Befriend, Not Fight or Flight." *Psychological Review* (2000), 107(3): 41-42.

Books

Apter, Terri and Josselson, Ruthellen. *Best Friends: The Pleasures and Perils of Girls' and Women's Friendships*. New York: Crown Publishers, 1998.

Brehony, Kathleen. *Living a Connected Life: Creating and Maintaining Relationships*. New York: Henry Holt, 2003.

Blanchard, Ken; Lacinak, Thad; Tomkins, Chuck; & Ballard, Jim. *Whale Done! The Power of Positive Relationships*. New York: Free Press, 2002.

Bronson, Po. *Why Do I Love These People? Honest and Amazing Stories of Real Families*. New York: Random House, 2006.

Forward, Susan. Toxic *Parents: Overcoming Their Hurtful Legacy and Reclaiming Your Life*. New York: Bantam Books, 2002.

Paul, Marla. *The Friendship Crisis: Finding, Making, and Keeping Friends When You're Not a Kid Anymore*. Emmaus, PA: Rodale, 2004.

Vaillant, George E. *Aging Well: Surprising Guideposts to a Happier Life from the Landmark Harvard Study of Adult Development*. Boston: Little Brown, 2002.

You can't sit back and wait for people to come to you.
You have to get out and do something,
even if it hurts.

From Betty's story

The men's group is good for talking things out.
It has been part of my learning about change.

From Fred's story

13

Two to Tango
Spouse or Partner

It was the best of times, it was the worst of times.
Charles Dickens

We often underestimate the impact on the other aspects of our lives, of making just one change. Nowhere is this truer than in our relationship with our spouse or partner. For example, we may now have the flexibility to work part time or from home. That change may alter how and when we want to spend time with our spouse. We may be lucky enough now to have more time and money to travel or to live in a new location, but our spouse may not share an interest in the same places. Unwittingly, we assume that when we are ready for change, our spouse is ready too, or that our spouse wants what we want.

It's difficult enough making changes in our own life, let alone meshing our plans with the life decisions and changes of our partner. Sometimes two people are going through life changes at roughly the same time. But often one person is ready for change while the other is content with life as it is. And, sometimes, staged change such as one partner retiring first is financially necessary.

For some couples the decisions made years ago, particularly those relating to work and children, are running their course. The children are grown or growing up, and one or both partners may be ready to do something different. Couples who decide to have children when one or both are in midlife, or who now need to assume the care of grandchildren, may also have partnership issues to work out.

Couples may have to cope with changes in their roles if one spouse is laid off, retires earlier than the other, or there is a reversal in which spouse is the primary income provider. Sometimes the household division of labor needs to change, too, and feelings may pop up that are harder to talk about than simply who takes out the garbage.

Signs of aging in our partner or ourselves such as changes in appearance or health may put us on an emotional roller coaster. Our feelings about our partner or ourselves may become negative. But, there can be a positive effect on the relationship we have with our partner if we show each other understanding about the fears and problems of aging.

Communication is the key to making this time of life the best of times. We shouldn't assume our partner shares our interests, goals, and attitudes about the future. Each of the following stories demonstrates the need for communication.

Working Together and Changing Roles—Tom's Story

Tom and his wife, Pat, lived in the same Minnesota community their entire lives. They lived in the house Tom's grandfather built, enjoying their work, family, and community. They were content. Until they serendipitously discovered what they wanted to do next, they didn't know they felt stagnant and wanted a change. While on vacation they discovered the small town of their dreams—the dreams they didn't even know they had. Within nine months Pat quit her job, Tom sold his business, and they sold their home in Minnesota. They bought a bed and breakfast (B & B) in their new hometown 2,000 miles from Minnesota.

Tom and Pat had always made decisions easily. Over their many years of marriage they tended to agree or at least to defer to each other. Throughout the entire process of moving, they were never frightened of the possible ramifications of their decision. Pat had had the germ of an idea for a B & B for years, and Tom was happy to go along with it. He says, "It was an idea Pat was in love with, and I'm in love with Pat." Each of them had appropriate skills for this venture. Tom had mechanical skills and was good at marketing and administration. Pat was great at multi-tasking in all the ways necessary to promote the comfort of their guests.

Problems surfaced after their first season at the B & B. Early on, they'd decided they would each choose their roles and be in charge of their own areas so they wouldn't bump into each other. But it wasn't working out. Somebody *had* to be in charge. They tried setting up formal meetings to work out their differences, but neither understood what the other wanted. Tom was "surprised at the strength of our feelings and how angry we were."

They finally determined that several issues were coming into play. They had underestimated the stress of such a major move. Each of them was in the process of redefining his or her identity and role in life; plus they had left their support system of friends and family in Minnesota. Tom had to come to grips with the fact that the B & B was Pat's dream. It wasn't his. Tom acknowledges, "The business, the brains, is Pat." Pat is now in charge, and Tom regards himself as her employee.

Tom realizes they still have some problems working together. As a couple they have different feelings than they would as unrelated co-workers. He still has problems deferring to Pat when she asks him to do something. "I just don't always want to do what she wants me to, when she wants me to do it." Tom is now focused on finding new interests that are just his own. He's taking cello lessons and looking for part-time work as a handyman. He also continues to maintain the website for the business he sold in Minnesota.

Lessons from Tom

Tom and Pat each had to develop new roles and figure out how to relate to each other in these new roles. Because their marriage was strong, they overestimated their compatibility for running a business together and underestimated the decision making it required.

> **!**
> 👁 Major life changes such as starting a business together may require that partners reexamine their roles and identities. It's critical that they share their feelings and openly communicate about problems.

While Tom and Pat both heartily agreed to their move, some couples have problems agreeing not only on a community and climate, but also on the size of a home.

Dreams of Leisure—Sheila's Story

Sheila, 52, works at an Ivy League university. She looks forward to more leisure time and money now that her sons have graduated from college. But, her idea of where she'd like to spend that time is quite different from her husband's. She wants to live without a car in a city such as New York or Boston and enjoy what cities have to offer. Her husband, John, dreams of living in Palm Springs. She admits that money will probably drive their decision, but fantasizes that "If we had a ton of money, maybe we'd have a little place in New York *and* in Palm Springs, and we could go between them." Luckily, Sheila and John have time for negotiation as well as time to accumulate the money they may need for a satisfactory compromise.

Lessons from Sheila

Sheila and John have very different dreams about where they'd like to live someday. Sheila realizes their dreams may be incompatible. Sheila and John need to start communicating now while there's time to plan and prepare for a compromise that will satisfy them both.

Sharing Space

Space is, or can become, an issue for couples when there's a change in their work routines, and one or both of them are home more. "Space" can mean how rooms or parts of rooms are used, or who has responsibility for a "domain" such as an office space or the kitchen. If a couple is "downsizing" to one car or one person begins using the family computer or phone line for a home-based business, problems can arise over who has priority access.

When one partner is at home more, he or she may want to engage in more joint activities or just need someone to talk to. The other partner, such as Barbara in the following story, may be uncomfortable with these changes.

Needing Her Own Space—Barbara's Story

Barbara's husband, Hank, gradually cut back his work hours over the five years prior to his full retirement. Barbara, who has always been a homemaker and active in her community, found that when Hank started spending more time at home "the most difficult thing for me was my space." It bothered her that someone else was there during the weekdays, something she wasn't used to. Barbara realized that her space issue was closely tied to how much time she had on her own. She says that sometimes she "just wanted him to go off alone. I like a few hours by myself."

Barbara and Hank have used his phased retirement to work out some of their differences. They experimented with solutions to their issues about time and space while he worked part time. She now enjoys the opportunities her husband's retirement has given them and has learned to be more spontaneous about how she uses her time. But she also advises that people, particularly women, "maintain their individuality" and independence.

Lessons from Barbara

Barbara and Hank's new relationship developed over time. Patterns that were established over many years weren't easy to change. They experimented with their issues of time and space and made changes gradually.

Work and Money

A relationship is also affected when a couple's income changes. With luck and careful planning some couples are able to maintain their lifestyle when one or both change jobs or retire and their income decreases. But many people want or need to continue working.

Some midlife job changes such as moving to another city may have an unanticipated downside for the partner not initiating the move. One partner may be "following their bliss" and find the perfect job. The other partner may have difficulty finding an acceptable job or adjusting to a new community.

> **!**
> ◉ Even with careful assessment before a job change or retirement, couples need to discuss frankly how the change will be accommodated and how it will affect both of them.

Renegotiating Relationships

As our lives change, we need to gain an understanding of ourselves as we currently are. We need to know what is important to us before we can effectively deal with relationship issues. For effective change to occur, we must have the self-knowledge to be confident in ourselves and in our abilities to cope with life.

All three stories in this chapter illustrate that knowing ourselves is necessary before a relationship can be successfully renegotiated. Tom and Pat found this out after they had changed their lives. Since then, they've gone through some rocky times figuring out what they want as individuals and how to adjust their relationship. Sheila and Barbara are both sorting out what they want as individuals. They both know that their ideas sometimes differ from their spouses.

Renegotiating relationships involves an ongoing assessment of individual *and* joint goals, boundaries, interests, and expectations.

> **!**
> ◉ As we change important roles, develop new identities, or alter our living space, we need to share our feelings and thoughts with our partner or spouse. *When the fixed patterns of our lives change, so do our relationships.* We need to talk with our partner or spouse about our individual goals and develop new goals as a couple.

Your Savvy Sisters' Advice

- Share your feelings. If you aren't accustomed to this, find a class, book, or counselor and bone up on your communication skills.

- Accept your differences and try compromise.
  Look for ways that both of you can meet your needs.
- Reach out to family and friends for support.
  They may have worked through similar, predictable
  life issues and can offer some tips.
- Let go of how you did things in the past if they don't
  work now.
- Listen, listen, and listen to your spouse or partner.

Couple's Planning

The following exercise provides an opportunity to identify
and discuss some of the predictable issues that crop up
for couples at midlife as they plan for their futures.

We suggest that you and your partner each complete
this exercise—or each just make notes on a blank sheet of
paper. After completion, schedule a time to talk about
each of your "Discussion Points."

Instructions:

1. Review the list of issues in the left column. Some of
   these may be areas of current disagreement with your
   partner; some may cause concern when you think
   about your future life with your partner. If you think
   of an issue that isn't listed, write it in a blank space
   at the end of the list.

2. Put a check in the "Current" box next to an issue
   if this is currently a problem between you and your
   spouse or partner.

3. If you need to discuss an issue with your partner
   or spouse because of changes you anticipate for the
   future, put a check in the "Future" box.

4. In the "Discussion Points" box, jot down the points
   you want to discuss with your spouse or partner.

exercise►

Couple's Planning

Issues	Current	Future	Discussion Points
Spending and saving money			
Time each of you wants to spend together			
Time each of you wants to spend on your own			
How rooms or spaces are used			
Household chores			
Daily schedules: mealtimes, bedtimes, etc.			
Individual boundaries: what each of you won't do			
If you have only one telephone line, computer, or car, when each of you have priority use			
Individual roles: who cooks, who makes travel plans, who handles the finances			
Individual domains: kitchen, office, workshop; when, how, or if a space is used by each of you			
Other			

Remember to set a time with your partner to go over the issues that may derail your relationship if they aren't discussed.

Resources to Help You and Your Partner Communicate about the Future

Books

Arp, David; Markham, Howard; and Stanley, Scott. *Empty Nesting: Reinventing Your Marriage When the Kids Leave Home.* San Francisco: Jossey-Bass, 2002.

Brody, Steven and Brody, Cathy. *Renew Your Marriage at Midlife.* NewYork: G.P. Putman's Sons, 1999.

Louden, Jennifer. *The Couple's Comfort Book: A Creative Guide for Renewing Passion, Pleasure and Commitment.* New York: Harper Collins, 2004.

Polston, Betty, with Golant, Susan. *Loving Midlife Marriage.* New York: John Wiley & Sons, Inc., 1999.

Savage, Elayne. *Breathing Room—Creating Space to Be a Couple.* Oakland: New Harbinger Publications, 2000.

Sheehy, Gail. *Sex and the Seasoned Woman: Pursuing the Passionate Life.* New York: Random House, 2006.

Shem, Samuel and Surrey, Janet. *We Have to Talk: Healing Dialogues Between Women and Men.* New York: Basic Books, 1998.

14

My Mother Lives in the Basement
Caring for Aging Parents

*Care for parents should not be a tiresome obligation;
the filial son and wife will do it with an appearance
of pleasure to make their parents feel at ease.*
Confucius

Not so long ago, as people aged and could no longer live
in their own homes, it was expected they would live with
one of their grown children. If sons or daughters couldn't
care for their parents, there weren't too many options
beyond nursing homes. Today there are considerably more
options for our elderly parents such as in-home care,
part-time companions, Meals-on-Wheels, or retirement
communities with facilities for retirement living, assisted
living, nursing care, and Alzheimer's care.

Even though fewer people today live in the same city
as their parents and fewer parents live with their adult
children, we may still bear considerable financial, logistical,
and emotional responsibility for our parents' care.

A joke we came across recently on the Internet identifies
a dilemma many adult children face with their parents:

At a nursing home in Albuquerque, a group of seniors was sitting around talking about their ailments. "My arms have gotten so weak, I can hardly lift a cup of coffee," said one.

"Yes, I know," said another. "My cataracts are so bad I can't even *see* my coffee."

"I couldn't even punch out the chad at election time, my hands are so crippled," volunteered a third.

"I can't turn my head because of the arthritis in my neck," said a fourth, to which several nodded weakly in agreement.

"I guess that's the price we pay for getting old," winced an old man as he slowly shook his head. The others nodded.

"Well, count your blessings," said one woman cheerfully, "and thank God, we can still *drive*."

The tables get turned as our parents age. We may find ourselves having to tell mom or dad that they can't have the car tonight; in fact, it's time for them to hang up the car keys for good. Their freedom and mobility will now be restricted.

> **!** As they age we may become our parents' parent. It's our turn to intervene and act in our parents' best interests. Generally, this doesn't happen all at once. It's a slow, not always smooth, process of role reversal.

As much as we want to help our parents, we may still be in the pressure cooker of managing our careers, running a household, financing our kids' education, and trying to plan our own eventual retirement. But if we are not clear about our parents' needs and expectations of us, as well as our ability to satisfy their expectations, we may feel guilty and frustrated. Also, unlike childcare that lessens over time, eldercare *increases* over time.

If we have a family of our own, our decisions about the best way to care for our parents may also affect our spouse or children. Communication is critical, but these are not easy conversations for parents or their adult children to have, as we find in Patrick's story.

Finding Solutions We Can All Live With— Patrick's Story

Patrick, 57, is a retired engineer. His sister has taken on the responsibility of caring for their 84-year old widowed mother. Patrick describes his mother as a dependent person who believes it's her daughter's duty to care for her—just like it was in the old country with three generations under one roof. But Patrick feels guilty. He wants to be a good son, not like his cousin who has seen his own mother only three times in 20 years. Patrick doesn't think the arrangement is fair to his sister. "I think I should take my mother off her hands from time to time," he says, "and we want her to feel welcome."

When Patrick retired from the government at 55, he and his wife built their dream house. Patrick designed it so "the downstairs is almost like an apartment." They thought it would be a good place for their children and grandchildren to stay when they visited. But Patrick admitted that he also created the basement apartment so that if something happened to his sister, it would be a place for his mother to live. But, he's not sure his wife, who just spent several years caring for her own mother until she died of cancer, would accept this arrangement.

Lessons from Patrick

Unfortunately, Patrick has never discussed the specifics of his plan for the basement apartment with either his wife or his mother. It may be that neither woman would be happy with the arrangement. Patrick needs to talk to them both, starting with his wife, about the obligation he feels to help with his mother's care.

Taking our parents into our home requires patience and good will on everyone's part. For all parties it may mean giving up some privacy and restricting space and time for possessions and friends. It may open unresolved parent/child issues or issues between our parent and our spouse. It's a commitment that, without boundaries, may go on indefinitely as our parents' health declines.

In *Are Your Parents Driving You Crazy?*, authors Joseph Ilardo and Carole Rothman provide a template for sorting out our parents' and our own needs and feelings.

For starters, do all parties acknowledge that a problem exists? If so, is the problem urgent? Ilardo and Rothman suggest trying to understand what's behind each party's behavior, including our own, and they encourage coming up with multiple solutions to find the one that comes closest to satisfying everyone.

Understanding Our Parents' Needs—Todd's Story

Todd, who was helping his frail 91-year old father prepare for a move from the family home to a retirement home, felt frustrated that his father wanted to keep his chain saw. They had limited time to sort out what would be taken to the retirement home, and Todd had mentally put the chain saw in the Goodwill pile. Then his father explained that he didn't see this as his last move; he still wanted to buy a cabin in the woods and would need the chain saw to clear brush. Todd knew this was unrealistic. But, once he understood what the chain saw meant to his father—that the retirement home wasn't the last move before he died—Todd rented a small storage space for these "symbolic" possessions.

Lessons from Todd

Listen to your parents. You may have one agenda or need, but they may have another. Sometimes both can be accommodated or compromises made.

Conversations with Our Parents—Valerie's Story

Ideally, the planning and conversations with our parents about the role we'll play as they age takes place far in advance of their need. These ongoing conversations must also include planning for our parents' death, and the adult children may need to start the conversation. For example, Valerie, whom you met in Chapter 5 about illness and loss, is an active 80-year old widow. When her husband died ten years ago and the family planned his memorial service, Valerie's daughter encouraged her to plan her own service as well.

Valerie, like many of our parents, didn't want to be a burden to her children. The conversation with her daughter about her memorial service motivated Valerie to make a series of decisions. She had her will updated, planned for housing in her declining years, and made sure her financial affairs were in order. "I did it mainly for my kids, not for me," Valerie says. "I want to be cremated; I have a plot. I've made it just about as easy for them as I can."

Lessons from Valerie

Valerie took the lead in making some crucial life decisions for herself, but if she hadn't, her daughter or another of Valerie's adult children may have had to prompt her. Valerie is in good health and will undoubtedly live a long time, but as she ages there may be additional decisions she hasn't foreseen—such as when to stop driving.

> **!**
> ◉ The dialogue with our parents about their needs and expectations must be ongoing.

exercise

Talk to Your Parents Checklist

Here is a checklist of issues to discuss with your parents
so that you know: 1) their needs and expectations, 2) the
necessary planning steps have been taken for their health
and comfort or in the event of their death, and 3) you have
the information you need to act on their behalf.

✔	Talk to Parents About
	Their wishes about their living situation such as remaining in their home vs. a retirement or assisted-living facility
	Services available to your parents where they live such as senior day care, Meals on Wheels, part-time companions, and home health care services
	Preparation of wills, including a living will, advance directives, and power of attorney
	Wishes concerning organ donation
	Planning of funeral, burial, or cremation
	Names of people to contact upon their death: attorney, financial advisor, CPA, friends, and associates
	Names and locations of banks and investment accounts, safety deposit box, life insurance policies, tax returns, and other important documents
	Wishes for distribution of personal items not identified in wills
	Other

Caring for the Caregiver—Maureen's Story

We've been talking about our parents' needs, but, as
caregivers, it's crucial that we identify and plan to take
care of our own needs.

Ken Dychtwald in *Age Power* describes the typical caregiver as a "45 to 55-year-old woman who works full time

and spends 18 hours per week caring for her 77-year-old mother." The contribution of time is significant. This level of emotional and time commitment leaves little time for a personal life, as Maureen discovered.

If Maureen were to run an ad in the personals column, it might read like this: "Woman in her 50s seeks a social support network beyond her mother and husband. Passionate about gardening, architecture, and the environment."

Maureen is at a crossroad. She and her husband sold their business, and she chose not to play a key role in a new one. Her husband, whom she describes as "high maintenance," is 13 years older than she is. He resists her attempts to separate from their shared professional life. Maureen's mother, who was once a strong and independent woman, lives with them and is showing signs of decline.

Maureen anticipates that being a caretaker will become a permanent part of her life, and she knows she can't do it alone. When she finishes being her mother's caretaker, she'll be her husband's. "By then it will be time for someone to be *my* caretaker," she says, and she questions who that will be. She doesn't want to burden her family or have them be the only source of her social life.

That's why Maureen wants to go back to school, study architecture, and form new relationships. "But it's difficult for my husband—he feels threatened," she says. "I don't know how it will go. I need to develop and expand my life and connections." She wants to be able to pick up the phone and know she can reach friends who share her interests. Maureen has never had many female friends or "been one for networking," but she finds she needs to make friends now.

Lessons from Maureen

Maureen has looked ahead and realizes she will be a caregiver for many years. She has wisely started to think about what she needs to keep her going such as friends and new interests. Refer to Chapter 12 on social ties for ideas on developing friendships.

> **!** 👁 It's a simple formula—if you don't take care of your emotional and physical well-being, you won't have the stamina to care for others. There is a paradoxical commitment/exhaustion ratio: *Those who are most committed and involved are most likely to become emotionally and physically exhausted.*

The Juggling Act for Working Caregivers

Juggling the demands of work, family, and caring for a parent can be more difficult and stressful than you ever expected. It's hard to take care of someone whose needs intensify and whose condition worsens. Add to this a lack of preparation and unrealistic expectations, and you can set yourself up for problems.

MetLife, in their 1999 "Juggling Act Study," predicted that by 2009 one in ten people who work would also be providing care for an elderly person. They predicted that most of those people would seriously underestimate the time required and the impact on their work. The study participants, 76 percent of whom were workingwomen, reported that they started out providing a small amount of care, but over time the obligation increased. A majority had anticipated that caregiving would last only one or two years, but they found that four or more years were required.

Caregivers found they often had to pass up a promotion, job relocation, work-related travel, or the opportunity to train for new skills because of their responsibilities. Some caregivers were forced to reduce their working hours or retire early. These factors led to losses in career advancement, salary, and retirement income.

The employers of caregivers are also affected. Employers say their employees' growing eldercare obligations result in lowered productivity and the increased costs of absenteeism, turnover, and early retirement. Yet, few companies have programs to support working caregivers.

If you don't anticipate and plan for all the costs associated with caring for your aging parents, you'll neglect other important aspects of your life.

Your Savvy Sisters' Advice

- Find an employer, if you're a working caregiver, who provides flexible working arrangements such as flextime, telecommuting, job-sharing, or compressed workweeks, e.g., four 10-hour days.
- Learn about your rights under the Family and Medical Leave Act (FMLA) to take time from work to care for a parent who is seriously ill.
- Develop or maintain a social and emotional support system beyond your family, and dedicate time each week for yourself.
- Involve your spouse, partner, and children in discussions about caring for parents in your home.
- Meet with siblings and siblings-in-law to plan for sharing the care for elderly parents.
- Budget for the expenses or loss of income that might result from caring for parents.

- Investigate purchasing long-term care insurance for yourself.
- Consider counseling if old parent/child issues emerge as you becoming more involved in your parents' lives.

Resources for Caring for Your Aging Parents

Books

Delehanty, Hugh and Ginzler, Elinor. *Caring for Your Parents: The Complete AARP Guide.* New York: Sterling Publishing, 2005.

Doka, Kenneth J. and Davidson, Joyce D. *Caregiving and Loss: Family Needs and Professional Responses.* Washington, D.C.: Hospice Foundation of American, 2001.

Dychtwald, Ken. *Age Power.* New York: Tarcher/Putnam, 1999. (See chap. 8, Intergenerational Relations.)

Ilardo, Joseph and Rothman, Carole. *Are Your Parents Driving You Crazy? How to Resolve the Most Common Dilemmas with Aging Parents.* Acton, MA: VanderWyk & Burnham, 2001.

LeBow, Grace and Kane, Barbara. *Coping With Your Difficult Older Parent: A Guide for Stressed Out Children.* New York: Avon, 1999.

Loverde, Joy. *The Complete Eldercare Planner: Where to Start, Which Questions to Ask, and How to Find Help.* New York: Times Books, 2000.

Morris, Virginia. *How to Care for Aging Parents.* New York: Workman Publishing 2004.

Piver, Susan. *The Hard Questions for Adult Children and Their Aging Parents.* New York: Gotham Books, 2004.

Rhodes, Linda. *Caregiving as Your Parents Age.* London: New American Library, 2005.

Silin, Peter. *Nursing Homes: The Family's Journey.*
   Baltimore: Johns Hopkins University Press, 2001.

Solie, David. *How to Say it to Seniors.* New York:
   Prentice Hall Press, 2004.

Williams, Gene G. *Caring for Your Aging Parents.*
   Lanham, MD: Taylor Trade Publishing, 2005.

Videos

The Educated Caregiver. 3-tape set produced by Lifeview
   Resources, available on Amazon.com.

Websites

- www.aarp.org/families
   Topics include caregiving, home design, legal issues,
   end of life. Online seminar on caring for parents.

- www.ec-online.net
   ElderCare Online

I need to develop and expand my life and connections.

From Maureen's story

Part Six

Pulling It All Together

The two chapters in Part Six are devoted to helping you successfully create a plan for your life after 50. You're already well on your way in your planning process.

In the preceding chapters we've tried to:

- Help you identify what's important to you now
- Prompt you to think about your future
- Point out strategies for making transitions at midlife
- Provide resources to get you started

It's time for you to pull together your ideas and write a plan. Chapter 15 is a summary of the key concepts we've covered. It directs you back to important exercises. Chapter 16 provides worksheets to get you started with *Your Life After 50 Plan*.

*Life after 50 can be a time of rejuvenation
rather than retirement.*

Part One

15

Your Savvy Sisters Summarize

Each chapter of *How to Create the Life You Want After 50* includes advice from your Savvy Sisters—tips and ideas from our research and from the people we interviewed for this book. For your convenience, we've summarized the ideas here by topic.

Use this summary to help develop *Your Life After 50 Plan* in Chapter 16.

Work

- Manage yourself. You are the person most qualified to manage your career.
- Figure out what you like to do and what you're good at. Find work—full time or part time, paid or unpaid—that requires the best you have to contribute.
- Complete the *Midlife Transitions Inventory* in Part Four to synthesize your decisions, experience, skills, knowledge, and priorities.
- Explore new interests that may lead to new work opportunities.

- Remember, small changes can have a significant impact on how you feel about your work.
- Use the *Work and Life Values Fit* exercise in Chapter 8 to make the transition from what you are currently doing to what you might do in the future.

Financial Security

- Identify your priorities and figure out what you need for financial security and independence.
- Determine what your resources are and develop an investment strategy.
- Track your progress.
- Use the *Current and Future Expenses and Income Worksheets* in Chapter 2.

Appearance and Fitness

- Recognize that everyone's body changes after 50.
- Keep active through lifelong learning, training, travel, work, stimulating daily activities, and relationships with other people.
- Increase your stamina with a positive outlook and enticing goals.
- Exercise, but remember to warm up first.
- Get hearing aids, glasses, etc., if you need them.
- Take the *Healthy Living Quiz* in Chapter 3, and address the issues it raises.

Place and Space

- Don't rush into a move.
- Rent first if trying out a new location.
- Try out a new location for four seasons before buying a home.

- Experiment with your needs for space. First try to reorganize your current space.
- Audit your current living space for its good and bad points for the future.
- Use the *Place Needs Inventory and Space Needs Quiz* in Chapter 4.

Health

- Take your health and fitness seriously, but, if you are ill, don't organize your life around your illness.
- Organize your life around health-promoting activities.
- Use your brain and body to keep them healthy. Use it or lose it!
- Learn to relax.
- Eat a nutritious diet; poor eating habits catch up with you.
- Use the *Memory Boosters* in Chapter 5.

The Transition Phase

- Find a method of personal reflection that suits you.
- Reassess your values—complete the *Midlife Values Inventory* in Chapter 6. What was important to you at 30 or 40 may not be as important at 50 or 60.

Optimism

- Learn how to be more optimistic. An optimistic point of view offers profound physical and mental benefits.
- Monitor your habitual thinking processes; what you tell yourself about events affects how you feel about them.

- Identify what you can control and what you can't. Don't waste your physical and emotional energy on things you can't control.
- Use the *Assessing Your Positive Attitude* exercise in Chapter 7.

Serving the Community

- Identify the skills and interests you want to use as a volunteer.
- Determine which benefits of volunteering are important to you.
- Define a volunteer position you want and how much time you can commit.
- Research the organizations that would be a good match for your interests and availability.
- Complete the *What Skills Do You Want to Use?* exercise and the *What Do You Want to Do?* quiz in Chapter 9.

Creativity and Learning

- Use your creativity. It increases your self-esteem and helps you reinvent yourself at midlife. It is an antidote to the fear of losing your identity if and when you leave your career.
- Learn to listen to your inner, creative voice. Try the *Encourage Your Creativity* and the *Listen to Your Inner Voice* exercises in Chapter 10.
- Experiment with new interests through classes and self-study.
- Explore taking courses or completing a degree for work or personal benefit.

Traveling

- Plan; you'll get more out of your experience—particularly if you're traveling with a companion.
- Get started. As you grow older, your options for travel may be reduced.
- Use the *Travel Daydreaming Quiz* and *Places to Visit / Things to Do* exercises in Chapter 11.

Friends and Family

- Appreciate your friends. People who have friends are happier and healthier than those who don't.
- Work at the friendships you want to maintain.
- Use or develop your listening skills.
- Focus on your friends' needs.
- Make new friends with both men and women of all ages.
- Complete the *Friendship Survey* in Chapter 12.

Spouse or Partner

- Appreciate your spouse or partner for his or her special place in your life.
- Let go of how you did things in the past, if they don't work now.
- Listen, and share your feelings.
- Accept your differences and try to compromise.
- Reach out to family, friends, or professional counselors for support.
- Consult the *Couple's Planning* exercise in Chapter 13.

Caring for Aging Parents

- Find an employer that provides flexible working hours.
- Develop a social and emotional support system beyond your family.
- Involve your spouse, partner, and children in discussions about caring for parents in your home.
- Meet with siblings and siblings-in-law to plan for sharing the care and costs for elderly parents.
- Identify your aging parents' needs and expectations. Use the *Talk to Your Parents Checklist* in Chapter 14 to guide your conversation.

16

Your Life After 50 Plan

To create the life you want after 50, you are much more likely to achieve your goals if you create a written plan to make it happen. You have already started to:

- Analyze the events or experiences that motivated you to begin this planning process
- Explore your transitions
- Identify your interests, skills, and strengths
- Examine the importance of relationships in your life

Now use the worksheets provided below to develop your plan. You may not want to make plans in every category right now—focus on the areas you are most excited about. You may need far more space than we've provided here. In fact, we encourage you to copy the categories into a notebook or your computer so you'll have all the space you need.

Remember, making plans is not a one-time activity. Make a note on your calendar to review and revise your plans, if only briefly, every year. Pick a date, such as your birthday, so your plan remains current.

Here are two examples to get you started. Notice that each of the 13 categories has three sections: Ideas, Action Steps, and Target Dates.

Example 1: Friends and Family

Ideas: I'd like to develop my circle of friends. What friend would I like to spend more time with? What attributes or interests would I like a new friend to have? What activity would help me meet such a person?

Action Steps: I'd like to spend more time with Jane, so I'll suggest that we meet for lunch once a month. I'd like to meet people who live close by, so I'll go to the neighborhood picnic. I'll also attend the coffee hour after church.

Target Dates: I'll call Jane this week. The picnic is on my calendar for next Saturday. I'll be at church on Sunday.

Example 2: Serving the Community

Ideas: I want to help children learn how to read.

Action Steps: I'll call the local elementary school and find out if they need help—or if they can suggest an organization. If they have a suggestion—and I like it— I'll schedule a visit. Otherwise, I'll check with the local volunteer referral organization.

Target Dates: Next week.

exercise▸

Your Life after 50 Plan

You're on your own now. For each category consider whether the actions you plan to take are in synch with the results of your *Midlife Values Inventory* and your *Midlife Transition Inventory*.

1. Work

Ideas:

Action Steps:

Target Dates:

2. Financial Security

Ideas:

Action Steps:

Target Dates:

3. Appearance and Fitness

Ideas:

Action Steps:

Target Dates

4. Place and Space

Ideas:

Action Steps:

Target Dates:

5. Health

Ideas:

Action Steps:

Target Dates:

6. The Transition Phase

Ideas:

Action Steps:

Target Dates:

7. Optimism

Ideas:

Action Steps:

Target Dates:

8. Serving the Community

Ideas:

Action Steps:

Target Dates:

9. Creativity and Learning

Ideas:

Action Steps:

Target Dates:

10. Traveling

Ideas:

Action Steps:

Target Dates:

11. Friends and Family

Ideas:

Action Steps:

Target Dates:

12. Spouse or Partner

Ideas:

Action Steps:

Target Dates:

13. Caring for Aging Parents

Ideas:

Action Steps:

Target Dates:

We, your Savvy Sisters, hope that *How to Create the Life You Want After 50* has inspired you to create a plan that will make your life all you want it to be. The future starts tomorrow; begin planning today!

About the Authors

Sara Brown, Ph. D. and Joan S. Malling are partners in Savvy Choices LLC, which provides midlife planning services for individuals and organizations. Joan and Sara complement each other in their expertise and style. Joan has over twenty years experience creating and developing professional development programs for mid-career adults. Sara has had an extensive career in the fields of human resource management, organization development, corporate coaching, and career planning for midlife professionals.

About Savvy Choices LLC

The goals of Savvy Choices LLC are:

- For individuals to become clear about the direction of their lives.
- For organizations to increase the productivity and commitment of their 50+ workforce.

Savvy Choices LLC offers workshops focusing on the choices and challenges people face at midlife. The goals of the workshops are to help participants gain perspective on midlife issues, learn positive methods for moving through life change, and create a plan for life after 50. The workshops are interactive with exercises, activities, and case studies.

To learn more about workshops, consulting, or individual coaching, see our website: www.savvychoices.com.

To order additional copies of
How to Create the Life You Want After 50
or a copy of the
Group Discussion Guide for
How to Create the Life You Want After 50,
contact us at www.savvychoices.com
or call 541-482-5561.